EGYPT
AND
THE SUDAN

# EGYPT
# AND
# THE  SUDAN

*Countries of the Nile*

Larry Henderson

THOMAS  NELSON  INC.
New York          Camden

Excerpts from *A History of Egypt,* by James Henry Breasted, have been reproduced with the permission of the publishers, Charles Scribner's Sons, to whom permission is gratefully acknowledged. They appear on pp. 45, 51, 60.

Photographs are by Larry Henderson with the exception of the following: pp. 8, 62, 70, 83, 120, 153, 167, 171, 189, Arab Information Center; pp. 16, 88, 107, 125, 135, 138, 144, 155, 158, 164, 174, 180, 183, 184, 187, 188, 193, 194, 196, 199, 205, 206, 208, 209, United Nations; p. 113, State Information Service; p. 136, UPI Radiophoto. Permission is gratefully acknowledged.

*First edition*

*Library of Congress Catalog Card Number: 70-140078*

ISBN 0–8407–7060–X (trade); 0–8407–7061–8 (library)

Manufactured in the United States of America

To my son Ross,
who accompanied me on my journeys
through Ancient and modern Egypt
and the Sudan

*Books by Larry Henderson:*

The Arab Middle East
Egypt and the Sudan
Vietnam and Countries of the Mekong

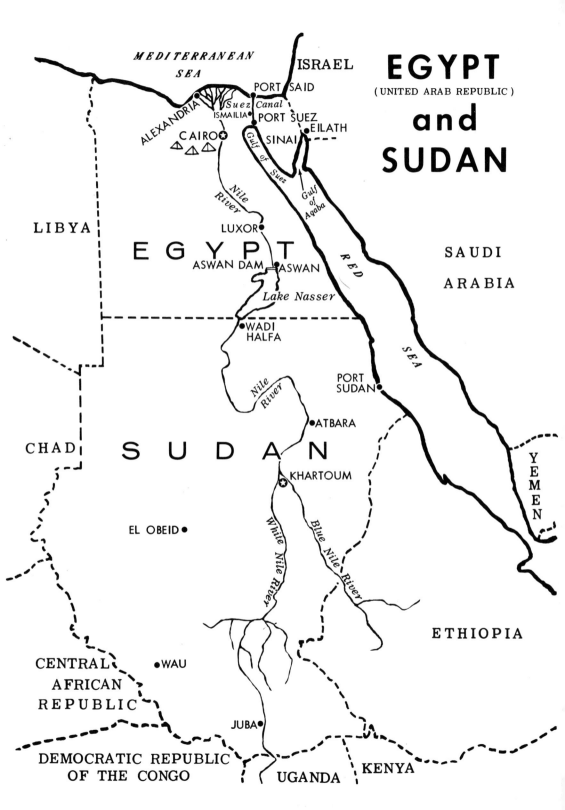

# Contents

*The Nile at Aswan.*

# PART I. EGYPT

# The Nile

## A Ribbon of Green

The main railway station at Cairo is an unprepossessing place to start any journey. Despite the presence of Rameses II in granite—65 tons, says your guide proudly—outside the entrance, the interior is likely to strike a gloomy note. A sea of humanity swirls around you—some seated in family groups, others staggering under enormous loads of luggage, all jostling, talking, or screaming, and generally behaving as if the end of the world were near.

If your journey begins at nighttime, the impression may be more fearsome still. Under wartime blackout regulations, no light may show in any government public building. This means you will have to make your way through this frantic mob accompanied by a porter carrying all your belongings, stepping over sleeping bodies, and through tunnels under the railway tracks, to reach your sleeper.

At last, safely ensconced in the corner of your carriage, a smiling waiter, in a swirling galabiya (a cotton tunic reaching to the ankle) and turban, will bring you tea and turn down your bed for the night. But still no lights may be turned on, and after the train pulls out of the station, you sit in the dark staring out the window at the pitch-black countryside. What sort of land is this? you wonder, feeling a little as if you had passed through the gates of the underworld, where, the ancient Egyptians believed, the jackal-headed god Anubis lay waiting for them.

Morning comes early, however, and the level rays of the sun wake you

*A Nile village in Egypt. Villages are built of mud bricks.*

from your slumber. You press your face to the window, and the endless panorama of the river valley passes before you. It is an incomparable scene. You have been transported from the turbulent, chaotic present into a biblical world of blazing sunlight, blue waters, mud-walled villages, and the ordered calm of a patriarchal society.

The train here follows the east bank of the river, or sometimes a canal fringed with rows of palm trees. In the foreground, the villages cluster under the umbrella of green, sometimes behind high walls of sunbaked mud—one-story, square structures, for the most part topped, here and there, by the minaret of a mosque, like a tall white pencil stabbing the morning blue. Beyond the villages lie fields of sugar cane, the broad river, and, in the distance, the black cliffs of the western escarpment holding back the sands of the desert.

For, with the exception of the huge Nile Delta, all inhabited Egypt is but a ribbon of green stretched across a bare and empty land. The valley of the Nile, usually five or six and never more than fifteen miles wide, contains some of the richest soil in the world, silt washed down by the annual spring floods from the mountains of Abyssinia (Ethiopia), for thousands of years. This life-bearing soil is contained between the walls of shell limestone, which mark the limits of fertility. Beyond, all is desert.

Here, in this narrow space, an early civilization was born and has continued without interruption for over five thousand years. The scene you see out of your train window is in most respects the same scene you would have glimpsed if you could turn back the clock in this valley a thousand, two thousand, or even five thousand years! Nowhere else in the world has such continuity existed. Your train window is a time machine, catapulting you back to the beginning of the civilized world.

Water buffalo stand chewing their cud, while men in the fields are bent double. Women carrying huge bundles of sugar cane on their heads stare back at you. On the station platforms, small groups of men squat in circles, eating their breakfast. Egrets, herons, and sometimes an ibis, sacred bird of ancient Egypt, sail by in the sky. All is calm, ordered— seemingly eternal.

In the distance, from time to time, pass the strange outlines of the pyramids of Sakkara, Dashur and Meidum—those huge, man-made

*Typical canal scene at Fayum.*

mountains of stone erected at the very beginning of the Egyptian civilization, all those years ago and still here today, an important part of life in the Nile Valley.

## Harnessing the Flood Waters

If you descend from the train, as you must in order to see the countryside, you will find yourself in a busy, pulsating world, where the daily tasks have changed little as the millennia go by. Here, as always, life still depends on the river, and in the management of this sleeping giant no one can equal the Egyptians.

For the principal labor of man in this valley has been to control the spring floods—to catch as much of this abundant water as possible and store it for the long dry season. Now, of course, the Aswan High Dam provides a more reliable source of water storage and supply; but the chief job for every farmer is still that of irrigating his own fields.

13

In former times this was done exclusively by a system of "basin irrigation." The water of the Nile is caught in man-made basins—great tracts of land that are dammed up with mud walls during the spring floods. The crops are sown in the newly deposited silt and harvested shortly after the water has dried up. The land then lies burned and dry until the next flood season.

Now that the Aswan Dam regulates the Nile waters more evenly throughout the year, the system is no longer widely used, especially since it was wasteful of land. During ancient times, the village population of Egypt was never more than two or three million. Today the peasant population is eighteen or nineteen million.

Perennial irrigation began in the last century to cultivate the cotton and sugar crops that have come to be Egypt's main export products. These crops grow during the season of the low Nile and hence cannot be grown on basin land. Perennial irrigation means lifting the water from the Nile and distributing it to a network of irrigation channels to all the fields that lie on either side, sometimes thirty feet above the river. There are today 12,000 miles of irrigation canals in Egypt, and over 5,000 miles of drainage canals. And to do all this, the patient Egyptian has relied over the years on little more than his own ingenuity and back-breaking labor. It is true that nowadays you will hear the putt-putt of a gasoline pump here and there along the way. But far and wide across the fields, the major work is being done by such devices as the *shaduf*, the *saquia*, and the Archimedes' screw.

Even on the walls of the tombs of Ancient Egypt, you will see paintings of patient Egyptians working the *shaduf*. It consists of a long wooden arm, pivoted between two wooden posts. The longest part of the arm is attached to a bucket on the end of a long rope; the short part of the arm carries a weight of stone or a ball of mud. Hundreds of thousands of these devices are set up by the side of the river. A peasant, or "fellah," pulls the bucket down until it dips in water and then lets go. The counter-weight lifts the bucket up and pours its precious water into an irrigation canal. It is very hard work. A man with a shaduf can irrigate about a quarter of an acre a day.

Sometimes you see a pair of bullocks beside the river, or even a bullock and a donkey, working in circles and turning a big wheel which is laid flat on the ground. This is a *saquia,* or waterwheel. The flat wheel is connected by cogs to a vertical wheel, to which are attached several pots. Each pot in turn is dipped into the river and at the top of its circuit is dumped out into a conduit leading to the field. A *saquia* worked by one animal can irrigate about five acres a day.

Both these instruments have been in use for three thousand or four thousand years. A later invention was the Archimedes' screw, which was the very latest thing when it was introduced by the famous Greek scientist about the year 200 B.C. The Archimedes' screw is a wooden cylinder with a helix, or spiral, inside and an axis at both ends, with a crank handle on the upper axis. It is mounted on two posts at an angle of thirty degrees to the horizontal. The bottom end dips into the water of the canal or river. By turning the crank at the other end, the water is spiraled up by the helix inside the cylinder and out into the irrigation ditch above. It is said two men can irrigate three quarters of an acre a day by this method.

## *The Fellahin*

The present cultivated area of Egypt is 5.8 million feddans (a feddan is approximately 1.4 acres), or roughly ten thousand square miles. Before the Revolution of 1952, there were about two thousand landowners with estates of more than two hundred feddans each. Now the largest holding is a hundred feddans. But the bulk of the peasants still live on approximately five feddans each, and many on less. One man and his family can cultivate up to five feddans without hired help. (This is one reason why the peasants want large families.) But if they have to pay the rent, five feddans will hardly suffice.

Nineteen million cultivators on less than six million feddans of land! But if this were equally divided among them, and if there were no rents to pay, the average holding would not be sufficient to support life adequately. So here in the placid fields along the Nile we meet the reality of poverty in Egypt. The fields are dotted with the figures of the fellahin, bent double over their *fas* or *mirath.* Not for them the luxury of mechanized farm equipment, although tractors are becoming available through the farm collectives.

The man with five feddans must do his own work, weeding and making the irrigation furrows with the short-handled *fas*, a triangular iron blade fitted to the handle at an angle of 120 degrees. Or he will be bowed over the handles of the *mirath*, a type of wooden plow, pulled by two bullocks, that dates back to Pharaonic times. It consists of a pointed iron socket fitted to the bottom of a wooden shaft three feet high, with double handlebars at the top. Hinged on to the iron socket at the bottom is the wooden blade that turns the earth. With his *mirath*, he can plow about half an acre a day, but the furrows are very shallow.

Down the road a piece, you will come to the village. Villages are thick as dates on a palm tree along the river. Fellahin all live in villages, which are often very large, with twelve thousand or so inhabitants. All the houses are built of mud bricks. There is none of that hostility here that the Westerner encounters in Cairo. Farmers and merchants exchange friendly nods of greeting with you, and a simple inquiry at any house is sure to lead to an enthusiastic invitation to come in. You should always accept.

*To reduce the danger of fire and unhealthy smoke in houses, villagers are being taught how to build simple stoves from bricks made of mud.*

The typical house consists of three rooms—the living room just inside the front door, a kitchen-bedroom off this, and a room for the animals at the back. The floor is earth. There is little furniture: some straw mats for sleeping; a small table a few inches off the ground, around which the family gathers cross-legged for meals; in the kitchen, a primus stove, a *tisht,* or iron tub, for bathing, and an earth oven where the housewife bakes her own flat Arabic bread, which is the staple diet.

Of course, if you are invited to visit the *omda,* or headman, you may find him in a much bigger house of stone or burnt brick, usually white-washed. And some of the houses have quaint decorations, depicting a journey to other lands, such as the house of *hadji,* a pilgrim who has been to Mecca. The shops in the main street are thronged with people, especially the tinsmith, the tailor, and the barber (the latter is in heavy demand for tooth-pulling and circumcision, as well as general doctoring).

The atmosphere is lively and friendly, for all its poverty. For it must be remembered that these people have lived in the same villages, in much the same way, continuously, for five thousand years. A fellah usually lives and dies in the village in which he was born. There is a calm acceptance of the hardships of this life, which has been endured by countless generations.

In his brown skullcap and blue or white galabiya, the fellah has a biblical dignity about him. "After all," he seems to say, "we are the people who built the pyramids." His wife, the fellaha, is more retiring. Hidden behind her long head veil, reaching to the knees, she keeps to her home. Yet she is no drudge. Everyone looks up to her and we are reminded that ancient Egyptian society was matriarchal.

Yet suffering, though stoically endured, cannot be hidden. In the doorways can be seen the weak and listless figures of men and women without hope, hunched over, eyes vacant. Many of them suffer from bilharziasis, a disease that afflicts a large proportion of the peasant population. Fellahin get it working with bare feet in the irrigation ditches. Bilharzia, a parasite worm that breeds in the Nile, enters the human body through cuts and abrasions in the body, causing injury through hemorrhage and tissue damage. The result is anemia and intense pain.

In the days of basin irrigation, the parasites were killed off as a

*Donkey transport is still more popular than motor transport in rural Egypt.*

result of the sun-baking to which the basin land was subjected between flood seasons. Since perennial irrigation became general, the parasitic population has multiplied and no method has been found to exterminate them or to immunize against them.

The answer to these trials has always been a deep philosophic resignation. The fellahin—and we must remember that they are the oldest continuous society in history—have learned not to expect too much in life and to make the most of what they have. In this sense, they are older and wiser than the people of the West, who, while improving their lot, have failed to find contentment.

This philosophic resignation is expressed in great religious devotion. Both in the Coptic villages, which are Christian, and the Moslem villages, which are centered around the mosque, religious observances are very strict. So is the moral code. The Egyptian fellahin are sexually moral people. Liquor drinking is strictly forbidden in the Koran, and the prohibition is enforced by village convention.

The other side of this proud philosophy of poverty is a natural gaiety. The fellahin love music and many a man sits in his doorway, playing his rebab, a single-string viol. At night, the whole family like to gather on the roof—most houses have an outside stairway leading to the roof—and there entertain each other with songs through the long, hot evenings under the stars.

This sense of continuity from the remote past to the present—a chain of human lives lived in the same place, in the same way, using the same tools, thinking the same thoughts for five or six thousand years—this is something of immense historical importance. Nowhere else has this phenomenon occurred. Great civilizations have arisen—in China, in the jungles of Cambodia, in India, in Mesopotamia, in Greece, in Rome, in Central America—and they have passed away, leaving behind in some cases great monuments, aqueducts, temples, palaces, frescoes, poetry, . . . but the people have vanished. Or, if they have not completely disappeared, their ethnic roots have been torn up; they have absorbed the blood of conquerors, acquired new ways, new languages, new arts, new notions of right and wrong, good and bad, beauty and ugliness, so as to become a completely new people, often living uncomprehendingly amid the ruins of their ancient past. Not so in Egypt.

Throughout all recorded history, the valley of the Nile has remained continuously inhabited, without a break, by a people of North African and East African origin. Already in the year 4241 B.C., they had taken

*A camel caravan on the way to market along the Nile.*

*A planting calendar, 3000 years old, on the walls of the temple of Karnak. It is accurate to 365.25 days a year.*

root in the valley and begun the work of civilization. We know that date so precisely because in that year their astronomers introduced a calendar of 365 days, beginning on the day when Sirius rose at sunrise—a calendar, by the way, which is still in use and which is far more accurate than any subsequent calendar had been until about two hundred years ago.

Apart from occasional invasions, which left their mark on the character of the great cities, like Cairo, the way of life that evolved among the people we now call fellahin remained serenely unaffected by the passage of time. Only in the present day, when the increase in population due to the benefits of modern medicine has created a crisis of overcrowding and resultant poverty, do we see a single tremor in the calm balance of Nilotic civilization. History shows no example of revolution among the fellahin in four thousand years.

To solve the mysteries of the past, we need only to look at the modern Egyptians around us as we travel along the dusty highways beside the great blue-green river, under the shadow of the escarpments that hold back the desert. And in order to understand the present social and economic life of these people who hold the key to stability in the Middle East today we may see the records of the past, preserved almost like new on the walls of the ancient monuments.

Emil Ludwig, in his great book *The Nile,* has given an unequaled picture, like a double-exposure photograph, of this combination of "then" and "now" in the Nile Valley. He shows us an Egyptian fellah taking his little son to see the royal tomb of an ancient Pharaoh. When the boy enters the subterranean sepulcher and looks at the still-brilliant paintings on the walls, depicting life as it was lived five thousand years ago, he claps his hands and bursts out laughing. For what does he find in this tomb of the Pharaoh? Everywhere he finds himself.

There is the shaduf, rising and falling on its hinge from everlasting to everlasting, to raise water—water—only that this shaduf does not creak or whine. All the land lies divided into strips between narrow ditches. The plough is a mere piece of wood guided by a rope; it has no iron nose yet, but there are the two handles, and there are the camels and asses too that he knows so well. Look how the boy is driving the sheep with a stick, to make them stamp in the seed, while another entices the leader on with grain. What are they doing there? Now look—that is the good wheat they are binding to the flail so that next year it will be as good. And there is the priest too, receiving the firstlings, just as he does at home. But why are they slaughtering the ox beside the new building? That is going to be the temple, the one we take the stones from when the watchman isn't looking, and they are making a sacrifice for it as we do for the new steam-pump.

The fellah is enjoying himself, nudging the child and pointing—now to the other side of the same picture. There is mother—can you see her?—weaving a basket of palm leaves like the one on the shelf at home. There are her wooden combs, there she is painting her eyebrows, that is her veil—there the fellah is having his own head shaved, and Ahmed is the barber . . .

# The Pyramid Builders

## Gizeh

A visit to the pyramids at Gizeh will take you only a twenty-minute drive out of Cairo by taxi, but you will be traveling five thousand years back in time. Some preparations are necessary, therefore, if you are to make the journey successfully. First of all, you will need a good guide. By this, I mean a guide who knows how to be silent as well as how to talk; he will know the best approach to make (the pyramids should be approached from the front, with the guardian sphinx in the foreground); and he will carry a stout stick with which to drive away all the other guides who cluster around the base of the great monuments like vultures ready to pounce.

But no matter how well prepared you are, the pyramids will take you unawares. There you are, in your rickety old taxi, lounging back talking or craning out the window, and saying impatiently, "Yes, but where are they?" And suddenly you find you are looking far too low down on the horizon. There, looming over your head, of a color hardly distinguishable from the gray-brown of the desert, is a man-made mountain, and not only one, but, as you soon will see, three.

They are not beautiful, as pictured on tourist posters, with the setting sun behind them and a palm tree in the foreground. They are brutal, crude, overwhelming. That is because of their colossal size—the tallest (Khufu's) is 481 feet high, with a base of 755 feet on the side. The individual blocks are no longer covered with smooth limestone, sloping up

*The eternal sphinx was carved out of the living rock about 2500* B.C.

to the peak, as in ancient times—except for a tiny remnant like a snow-peak on the second pyramid, Chephren's. This valuable surface has long ago been stripped away by robbers. What remains is the skeleton of solid stone blocks each weighing 2½ tons, rising upward in tiers like a giant stairway.

The guide is telling you how this was done: the labor of a hundred thousand men working for twenty years . . . the blocks cut out of the quarries on the east side of the Nile—that is, across the river—and floated across the valley at high water to the base of the pyramid hill . . . then the erection of an enormous stone ramp, or causeway, up which the stones were dragged . . . and all this without a crane! It is a thought too awesome to be comfortable.

Then you are invited to *enter* the pyramid. For this entire monument was designed to preserve the body of one man—the Pharaoh—for all eternity. The entrance was located on the eighteenth course of masonry—or step—and so cunningly concealed that the massive block shows not a joint of one ten-thousandth of an inch. "Optician's work" the guide calls it.

Inside, some of the passages originally had been closed with port-cullises of granite. Up and down they lead and you walk hunched over (it seems they were small people, too, those ancient Egyptians), until at last you reach the sepulchral chamber. And there you find—nothing. In ancient times, your guide tells you, the tomb was rifled and the body of the king desecrated and its remains scattered. The man-made mountain was a failure.

Or was it? Can we be sure that this chamber is the real royal burial chamber, and not a false chamber designed to fool the robbers (and us) into thinking the tomb had already been robbed, and so to induce us to give up the search? That the Pharaohs have resorted to such trickery before we know from exploring other tombs filled with false shafts, make-believe coffins, and so forth, all designed to outwit future generations.

If so, there must be another chamber hidden somewhere in this mountain of stone. But how to find it? Who can move all these blocks and dismantle the work of five thousand years ago, even to find a

*The pyramid of Chephren at Gizeh. The entire pyramid was once covered with limestone facing, of which a fragment survives at the top.*

Pharaoh's tomb? Recently, Egyptologists have called science to their aid.

In the neighboring pyramid of Chephren (also apparently robbed of its royal owner long ago) an experiment was begun in 1968. Using a cosmic-ray detector to reveal any unknown hollow spaces, the experiment is based on the following principle: Since the pyramid is in exact geometrical proportions, correct to one ten-thousandth of an inch, each side should be penetrated equally by the rays from outer space. If there were any vaults or open space, they would let in more rays than the solid areas, thereby revealing their existence. So one million dollars' worth of detection equipment has been installed in the heart of the pyramid.

Their recordings have been fed into the IBM 1130 computer at Ein Shams University near Cairo. But the results have been singularly disappointing. No two recording patterns are the same from one day to the

*Model of Egyptian soldiers from ancient tombs. They carry bronzed-tipped lances. The Pharaohs placed these models in their tombs for protection in the afterlife.*

next. Either the geometry of the pyramid is in substantial error, or there is a mystery here beyond comprehension—some force that defies the laws of science at work in the pyramids. Egyptians are quick to recall that the Pharaohs placed a curse on all who would disturb their eternal rest. Perhaps the curse is still working.

## Life and Death in Ancient Egypt

Nevertheless, the tombs of the Pharaohs have yielded up a treasure far more valuable than their personal remains. They have preserved for us a record of their civilization so detailed and exact that we know more about the life of five thousand years ago than we do about much more recent times. This is because the Ancient Egyptians reconstructed their own lives in models, in carved figures, and in paintings on the walls of their tombs so that they could enjoy the things they loved even after death.

The cult of death in Ancient Egypt was really a cult of life—these Pharaohs enjoyed everything so immensely that they could not bear to leave it all behind, and so there sprang up the curious but very touching belief that everything in the objective world had its shadow image in another world. By surrounding the body of the departed with pictures, or ideographs, of their favorite wives, servants, dogs and horses, food and clothing, of hunting expeditions among the reeds of the Delta, conquests of black Nubians in the upper reaches of the Nile, these agreeable friends and pastimes would be projected into the afterlife. Thus the most terrible injury that could be done to the dead, apart from the destruction of the corpse itself—which apparently would then cease to exist in the other world—would be to damage or erase the shadow images on the walls of the tombs. Think how awkward it would be if the King's chief archers had the strings of their bows broken, or the spearmen lost the heads to their spears, or the King himself suffered the loss of his eyes. It is a fact that enemies of the Pharaoh actually inflicted these indignities on the tomb pictures in an effort to vent their malice in the afterlife!

It is because of these tomb pictures that we know so much about the life in the Nile Valley five thousand years ago. We know, for instance, that there was already an elaborate palace etiquette in those remote times, with many ranks of courtiers and every possible nicety of precedence. There was a lord of the royal wigs, a lord of the laundry, a lord of the wardrobe . . . one calls himself (in the hieroglyphic script) "overseer of the royal cosmetic box, overseer of the cosmetic pencil, chief sandal bearer to the King."

The houses of the rich men were, even in that remote time, large and comfortable. Methen, a noble of the Third Dynasty, built himself a house over 330 feet square. The materials were wood and sun-dried brick; there were many windows with shutters to keep out the sun and wind, with bright hangings, for protection against sandstorms. Beds, chairs, stools, and chests of ebony, inlaid with ivory of the finest craftsmanship, provided luxurious comfort. Tables had not come into use yet, but there were jars of alabaster, copper, silver, and gold standing about the floor. The floors themselves were covered with heavy rugs, on which people sat as they still do in the East. Outside, in the garden, the nobles spent their leisure hours beside a swimming pool, under the palm and sycamore trees, playing at checkers or listening to the music of the harp or the lute, while the children played ball.

And what of the working-class people—how did they live? Their low mud-brick houses, covered with thatch, were crowded together, wall to wall, in unbelievable slums. For furniture, the workman possessed a stool or two, a box, and a few potting jars. Then there were the barracks of the workmen who were pressed into service on one of the big state projects, as the building of a pyramid. These consisted of an immense succession of mud-brick rooms under one roof, with a long corridor running down the length of the building. On the farming estates, life for the workers was better, their living quarters less congested. It was not what our union leaders would commend as adequate labor conditions—yet we must remember that, at that time, the rest of mankind had scarcely emerged from the caves.

## A Man-made Mountain of Stone

This period, known as the Old Kingdom, is one of the most remarkable periods in history—remarkable for its cultural advancement, its social poise, and the grandeur of its creations, especially the pyramids. The astonishing, inexplicable thing is that it came at the very beginning of Egyptian history. Of course, there were times of even greater glory still to come in Egypt. But never again was there such a perfect harmony of civilization as in the Old Kingdom, and never again did men build pyramids.

Perhaps we shall never know how this came about. It is reasonable to suppose that many centuries of experimentation preceded the Old Kingdom, during which the skills required to build a great kingdom were developed. All we know is that at one point a man named Menes united the two kingdoms of Upper and Lower Egypt under one crown. He made his capital at Memphis, not far from present-day Cairo. His successors, Khufu (Cheops), Khafre (Chephren), and Menkure (Mycerinus), brought this ancient civilization to its full flowering.

Then something happened. Perhaps it was the "curse of the pyramids," which came to plague their own builders. Certainly there was something very strange about this fixation for pyramid building. Khufu was the first to become enslaved by the idea. It was said his father Re, the sun-god, revealed it to him in a dream: a house touching heaven, built for all eternity. In this house he should have everything needful after death, and each day his spirit would accompany his divine parent on his celestial journey around the world.

Khufu set about realizing the dream in earnest. Other Pharaohs had built tombs. Khufu would build a mountain. And he did, using up the intellectual skills, manpower, and physical resources of the nation for an entire generation to accomplish it. When it was done, the sense of accomplishment must have been overwhelming to every Egyptian at the sight of what man had done for the first time on this earth. And they all must have been very glad it was over.

But it wasn't over. No sooner had Khufu been ceremoniously sealed with all his wealth in his man-mountain than his successors set about building *their* resting places. Khafre erected an equally imposing mountain, alongside Khufu's. And after him, Menkure issued the same grim orders for more granite, more slaves, more building. Where was it all going to end? There is something frightening, almost mad, about this obsession, which was clearly going to crush the Egyptian people under

*Egyptian guide stands outside the tunnel into the royal tomb in the heart of the pyramid of Chephren.*

29

the weight of its own pyramids. The entire nation, generation after generation, was mobilized for one project: the Pharaoh's tomb. It is a significant comment on the power of the Pharaoh at this early stage of history that all of Egypt was his private estate, to be used in this way. But like all such dreams, it became a nightmare.

Already we can see the end approaching when we look at the third pyramid at Gizeh. Menkure's mountain is less than half as high as his predecessors'; its temple (for each tomb had its temple, where offerings were made to the Pharaoh as to a god) was faced with sun-dried bricks instead of granite. Perhaps the royal treasury was exhausted. Perhaps the people, grown sullen under the lash for so many years, had rebelled. But the fact remains that no Pharaoh ever built himself a pyramid again.

In fact, within a few hundred years, the Old Kingdom was in dissolution. History stops recording the names of the short-lived Pharaohs who vied with one another for power. Meanwhile the real power had passed to the nobles, each of whom became a despot in his own city or estate. It was a time of anarchy, in which all the progress of the first one thousand years of civilization seemed to have been lost.

Memphis, the world's first great city, was destroyed, never to rise again. Sometimes the noble warlords even posed as the "protectors" of their people, like the one who had inscribed on his tomb: "I rescued my city in the day of violence from the terrors of the royal house."

## Osiris and Set

When we look for the cause of decay so early in Egypt's long history, we must examine the cult of the priests. According to an Egyptian folktale, Khufu was one day enjoying an idle hour with his family when a seer asked for admittance to the palace. Summoned before Khufu, he told the Pharaoh that three children born to the wife of a certain priest of Re were really the children of Re and would therefore become kings of Egypt. Khufu looked very grave at hearing this, realizing it meant the end of his dynasty. And the seer added, reassuringly, "Thy son, his son, and then one of them shall rule." And that's just how it turned out.

What the folktale reveals to the amateur detective is an obvious

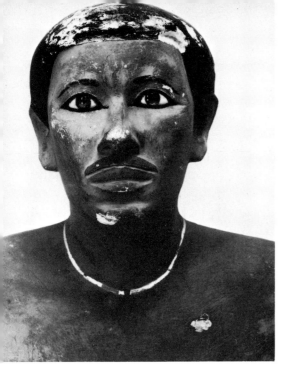

plot on the part of the priests to take over the kingdom in the name of Re. Already the Pharaoh was supposed to be the son of Re, the king of the gods, and hence the god himself. Now the priests were going to get into the act. The struggle for power between the Pharaoh and the priests continued throughout the history of Ancient Egypt, although in public they were united in their submission to Re. Whatever was done in Egypt was done in the name of Re, but whether the throne or the temple represented Re was the subject of a constant secret war.

In a sense this was a reflection of the war of the gods. If you talked to an Egyptian of the first, second, or third millennium B.C. about the "other world," he would give you a circumstantial account of this war. It all began when Osiris reigned as sun-god. In a land where the sun shone every day, his worship was universal. Every morning, he mounted his bark and sailed across the sky. This happy state of affairs was interrupted when Osiris was killed by his craftier brother, Set, who cut up his body into fourteen pieces and scattered them.

Isis, the faithful wife of Osiris, set out in search of her husband's

31

body. Gathering it up piece by piece, she embalmed the whole and by breathing into it she brought him back to life. It was impossible for him to resume his earthly life, however, so he became lord of the underworld. Meanwhile, Isis gave birth to a son, Horus, whom she hid in the marshes, as Moses was hidden among the bulrushes. When he was grown to manhood, Horus pursued Set, the god of darkness, and in a great battle that raged all over the land, he defeated the evil Set, and then mounted the throne of his father.

From Horus, the god of light, our ancient Egyptian informant would tell us, all the Pharaohs of Egypt are descended. In Upper Egypt, they wore the symbol of the hawk, which stood for Horus. In Lower Egypt, they wore the solar orb itself, when the sun-god was known as Re. The people loved this story; it absorbed a good deal of their time—thinking about it, talking about it, and fitting themselves into it. Isis was the true type of wife and mother, and the people loved to dwell on this goddess in their thoughts. Horus was the embodiment of a good son, and in him they always saw the triumph of justice and right.

The priests took over these folktales and organized them into the

*Statuette in wood from one of the ancient tombs.*

32

monumental worship of the dead that came to absorb and dominate all ancient Egyptian history. First came the embalming of the dead, following the example of Isis. Embalming became a massive industry in Egypt; the sellers of aromatic spices and preservatives, the manufacturers of coffins and tomb furniture outnumbered all other trades. Then came the building of the necropolises, the cities of the dead, in which every family had a tomb, a miniature pyramid, equipped and furnished just like the real house, sometimes much better, in which the ancestors continued their daily lives surrounded by every comfort and convenience. And at the top of the social pyramid stood the Pharaoh, the living embodiment of Horus-Re, the light of the sun.

But all this took time, thousands of years, before the cult actually crushed Egypt under its sheer weight. Already in the Old Kingdom, however, came the first of these shock waves when the power of the priesthood and the power of the king collided in a struggle to the death, reenacting the fight between Osiris and Set. The winner always became Horus and reigned in splendor, with the sun disk on his crown and the hawk on his shoulder. But behind the mask we see the faces of many different kinds of men (and even women), some strong, some warlike, some patriotic, some effeminate—all claiming to be Horus-Re. It is the greatest act of imposture known in history and it went on for three thousand years. How completely was it believed by the people? How much did the perpetrators themselves believe it? No one knows.

All we know is that from approximately 2750 B.C. to 2000 B.C., there occurred an enormous dark age called the First Time of Troubles. Set murdered Osiris over and over again, Horus triumphed over Set, only to be murdered in his turn, until, shivering and shuddering, the land of Egypt began its venture into civilization anew. When history resumes, the new capital is Thebes in Upper Egypt, known today as Luxor.

# The Secret Valley

## Luxor

The time to visit Luxor is winter. In February all the gardens along the river drive are in bloom with roses, shaded by rows of ancient phoenix palms. The walls of the private villas and the white luxury hotels are splashed with red bougainvilleas, and everything appears eternal summer under a cloudless heaven. Later, in April and May, it will be summer indeed; the temperature will rise to 110 degrees at noon, and the khamsin, a hot wind, will blow in from the desert, transforming the land into something like a furnace. This desert wind, which sometimes blows at sixty-five miles an hour, drives the sand before it in clouds that darken the sun.

But the Egyptian who lives here in all seasons must endure all things. Perhaps that is why the town of Luxor seems so sleepy by day and only comes to life at evening. By custom, in Upper Egypt the stores open from 8 A.M. till noon, and again in the evenings. Banks can hardly be induced to open at all; their closing time is 11:30 A.M. The exception is Tuesday—market day. Then the shepherds take over the town, filling the streets with their cries, or squatting patiently, surrounded by their flocks of sheep, donkeys, and camels, awaiting buyers. But for the rest of the week, Luxor returns to its ancient somnolence.

An air of strain and anxiety hangs over the town today, for Luxor has lived for many years on its reputation as a winter resort. Now the flood of wealthy pashas, coming to spend their winters complete with

*Colossal statue of Rameses II at Karnak shows the Pharaoh's wife standing between his feet. Wife's reduced scale indicates her relative importance.*

*Boarding the ferry at Luxor to the Valley of the Kings across the Nile.*

family retainers, has dwindled. Since the Revolution of 1952, the great landowners have been deprived of their income, and the villas they maintained along the waterfront are crumbling into ruins. The tourist trade, too, shaken by the constant barrage of gunfire, and of war talk in the Middle East, has moved on elsewhere. The guides and travel agents have a hungry look about them and shake their heads sadly and sigh for the "good old days."

But a new career has begun for Luxor as a center of archaeological interest. From all over the world, the devotees of archaeology converge and fill the gaunt, red-carpeted lobbies and Victorian dining rooms of the last-century hotels with serious-minded gossip about "finds," "periods," and "strata." They take off in the morning in horse-drawn buggies (another legacy of the vanished pashas!) armed with note-books, tape measures, and pocket telescopes, to investigate the nearby ruins of Karnak. Or they board the ancient riverboat, with its single-horse-power engine, to cross to the great necropolis on the other side of the Nile, where the bodies of lost Pharaohs still lie buried in the secret Valley of the Kings.

## The Rosetta Stone

Digging up the past has acquired an extraordinary fascination. In this age of encyclopedic knowledge, archaeology is still one of the great unexplored frontiers. Thanks to the archaeologists, we have learned more about Ancient Egypt in the past fifty years than in all the years that went before. It is a fact that until the discovery of the Rosetta Stone in 1799, almost nothing was known at all.

For the basis of all historical knowledge is the written record, and the key to Ancient Egyptian records was lost when, at the beginning of the Christian era, the last man died who knew how to read or write the Ancient Egyptian script, or hieroglyphics. Until 1799, the events of the world's first civilization remained virtually unknown, except for snippets in the writings of ancient Greek and Roman historians.

*The Museum of Cairo houses the treasures of Tutenkhamon and other Pharaohs.*

Then the mysterious stone, now in the British Museum, was unearthed near Rosetta by soldiers of the French Expeditionary Force. This stone bore an inscription in three different languages: hieroglyphics, debased Egyptian, and Greek. The French archaeologist Jean François Champollion deciphered the hieroglyphics by comparing the symbols with the other two known languages. It was found that these strange pictures of birds, implements, and parts of the body were really a picture language. At last, monuments, tombs, and temples could be dated, and their stories interpreted. The work was undertaken by another French Egyptologist, Gaston Maspero. He was the builder of the Museum at Cairo, and his name has been given to one of the principal streets in the capital.

## The Valley of the Kings

But still there were enormous gaps left in our knowledge. Where, for instance, were the remains of fifty Pharaohs whose graves had been found but whose bodies had been removed by robbers? Digging in Egypt became more and more like a detective story, especially as the quarry was likely to be wrapped in gold and covered in precious stones. And the mystery was deliberately planned by the ancient Pharaohs themselves, who had attempted to outwit the robbers by concealing their bodies in a secret valley across the river from ancient Thebes (Luxor).

No mystery story can equal this one—the cunning of the best minds of four thousand years ago pitted against the skill, experience, and equipment of the modern archaeologist. The "plot" is simple. How to conceal a body so that it may never be dug up. (As we have seen, this was essential to its future life after death.) Even in the earliest times, the Pharaohs found that the custom of burial, surrounded by all the wealth of a mighty king, presented too great a temptation to people. That was why Khufu built his great pyramid—to make it impossible for any robber to reach his body. He failed. All the pyramids were rifled in antiquity, especially after the Old Kingdom had begun to fall apart. Who could guard against such things through all eternity?

When peace was restored and the Pharaohs of Thebes held sway throughout the land, new ways had to be found. Instead of building a pyramid, each Pharaoh sought to select a hiding place for his body.

*Looking over the Nile to Luxor. In the mountains beyond is the famous Valley of the Kings.*

Where better than in the grim, lonely limestone mountains opposite Thebes?

In the dead of night, workmen were employed digging out tunnels in the mountainside: false entrances, blind alleys, hidden drops, every device was used to confuse and mislead any possible interlopers. In some cases, it seems, the workmen may have been put to death on completion of their task, so they should not talk. Only a very few were in on the secret—the priests. But, it seems, even they could be bought. With grief, Pharaoh after Pharaoh found the tombs of his ancestors broken into and plundered. Yet many of these priests were faithful.

The record of their desperate loyalty was discovered as recently as 1871, when an Egyptian thief, running from the police, took refuge in a cave, which he found contained the bodies of thirty-six Pharaohs! The thief, Abdul-rasul, tried to keep the secret and swore his whole family to it so they could extract the wealth and sell it piece by piece.

But Maspero's detectives caught him and the cache was uncovered. The explanation was part of a priestly effort to outwit the robbers by removing the bodies themselves, so as to leave the original tombs empty, and moving the bodies nightly from place to place, to preserve the Pharaohs from despoliation. And they succeeded—for almost four thousand years! Yet still many tombs have yet to be uncovered, and the work goes on in the Valley of the Kings.

This work is living history, and there is no better way to study it than by embarking on the launch at Luxor, manned by the turbaned boatmen in white and blue galabiyas, and visit the sites yourself. On the west bank of the Nile, old and dilapidated taxis are drawn up on the jetty, ready to take you into the rose-red limestone hills that front the great Western Desert.

## The City of the Dead

No matter what time of year, it is hot over here. Not a tree grows, though along the waterfront, where the annual inundation of the Nile has taken place for thousands of years, the fellahin are bent double in

*The Valley of the Kings. In these hills were concealed the tombs of over fifty Pharaohs. Modern street lighting helps to keep away robbers.*

*The tomb of Rameses IX in the Valley of the Kings. Original tombs were concealed in the mountain and were the object of intensive search by robbers and archaeologists.*

the fields, working on their sugar crop. The road—now well paved—twists and winds through the hills until it uncoils into a deep valley, running parallel to the river, but concealed from it by the first range of hills. The mountainsides are completely bare, and strewn with the rubble of innumerable rock falls. An ideal place for hidden treasure—or for robbers. As a matter of fact, searchlights play on the mountainsides all night to guard against unauthorized theft. Police stations, in well-defended blockhouses ringed with barbed wire, keep watch along the way.

At a certain junction, you must leave the car and walk. Here the hillsides on either side are honeycombed with gaping black holes about eight feet square. These are the entrances to the tombs. Before each one is a small neat sign bearing the name of a Pharaoh: Seti 1, Rameses II, Rameses VI, Rameses IX, Tutenkhamon . . . the City of the Dead.

When you plunge into the darkness of one of these tombs, you have the sensation of taking part in a mystery: the mystery of the hidden sepulchers, and the mystery of the cult of death itself. Down, down

Mummified head of Tutenkhamon. This boy Pharaoh died young, but his tomb is one of the best preserved ever discovered.

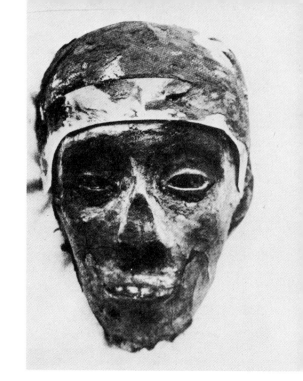

Tutenkhamon's tomb. The body is shown under glass in the original sarcophagus. Wall paintings show various episodes in the afterlife.

slopes the wooden ramp under your feet, sometimes for half a mile into the mountainside. Here you meet a deep well over which a plank is cast. This may have served to drain the tomb in case of floodwaters, and also to deceive robbers into taking it for the real entrance to the tomb. Doors broken through what seemed to be solid rock lead on at last to the burial chamber. Or is it the true one? You find yourself in a big empty room designed to look like a burial chamber that has been abandoned and left unoccupied. Here the would-be robbers might conclude the whole tomb was a "blind," and the Pharaoh might be buried in another place altogether. But in the floor is a false stone which, when lifted, leads to a stairway down to yet another chamber, where the great stone sarcophagus still stands.

They are all empty, these sarcophagi, because they were either rifled by robbers looking for gold, or by the priests who moved the bodies to protect them from desecration. The gold and silver, the tomb furniture, the thrones and chariots and hunting spears and little comforts provided for the afterlife—all are gone. But the paintings on walls and ceiling are still there, the gold shining like new—the scenes of court life, the Pharaoh's favorite horses, his falcon, his lion hunt, his victories over his enemies, all the pleasures and triumphs of his reign are recorded for us to see.

And more—here are his adventures in the afterlife, the journey to the Underworld, showing how he is stopped forty-two times by fierce demons who demand answers to riddles. Every Egyptian had to memorize these answers; they were written down in a handy little book sold by the priests—a tidy bit of priestly business. And then, at last, Pharaoh approaches the Judgment Hall, where Osiris awaits him, enthroned with forty-two assistant judges beside him. To each of the judges Pharaoh must plead "not guilty" to a certain sin, while his heart is weighed in the balances over against a feather, the symbol of truth. The forty-two sins are the same ones we would condemn today, such as murder, theft, slander, sexual impurity, adultery, blasphemy, and so on. For the first time in the history of the world, the idea of human accountability in eternity had been conceived. Those who pass the tests join Osiris in his sun boat as he sails through the heavens. The wicked are torn into pieces and flung back into the darkness of the tomb. Of course, Pharaoh invariably passed the test and became a god like his father Re, the sun.

These kings we meet here in the secret valley are quite different from those who built the pyramids at Gizeh. The Pharaohs of Thebes, who flourished in the Twelfth Dynasty, are much more civilized, urbane human beings. They are powerful and command great armies of soldiers and officials. But they do not rule alone. After the fall of the Old Kingdom, the local feudal lords took over the country, and they never quite gave it back. Now these lords, or "nomarchs" (from "nome," a province of Ancient Egypt), continued to act as the Pharaoh's vassals. But they did not reside at court. They had a life of their own. They even quarried out their own tombs in a corner of the red sandstone mountain (the Valley of the Nobles). Many were proud of their achievements. "I was one," wrote a nomarch on his tomb, "having goodly gardens and tall sycamore trees. I built a wide house in my city, and I excavated a tomb in my cemetery cliff. I made a canal for my city and I ferried people over in a boat. I was one ready for service leading my peasants until the coming of the day when it was well with me" (the day of death).

## A Golden Age of Arts and Crafts

The country was becoming wealthy, and a middle class had evolved to share in the wealth. Arts and crafts began to flourish, producing jewelry so exquisite that one American critic has said that "little ever produced later by the goldsmiths of Europe can surpass it either in beauty or workmanship." And, this was still two thousand years before Christ, when Greece and Rome were unheard of, and men were roaming Europe and Asia clad in animal skins!

But, as in all history, progress is made in a series of leaps forward, interspersed by periods of frightful ruin. Egypt had already experienced one of these, after the dissolution of the Old Kingdom. Now something similar was about to overtake the Middle Kingdom. For those who like to ask the eternal question—why?—it is not easy to find the answers. All was well in the Middle Kingdom; the wealth was better divided between all classes; justice was done in an exemplary fashion; and the

Pharaohs of the Twelfth Dynasty, men like Amenemhet I, and Sesostris I, II and III, were enlightened monarchs who deserved to be remembered for their good deeds. What was the flaw in this ideal society?

Perhaps the answer is constant throughout all time: jealousy. Jealousy of another's goods, another's power or success has deflected the course of human history more than any other single factor. Even the great Amenemhet I, founder of the dynasty, could not sleep peacefully at night. "None was hungry in my years," he said, "none thirsted then, men dwelt in peace, through that which I wrought." Yet he was attacked by members of his own household in the night and escaped only after a fight to the death in his bedroom. Sadly the old king warned his son, Sesostris:

> "Harken to that which I say to thee—
> Fill not thy heart with a brother,
> Know not a friend,
> Nor make for thyself intimates,
> Wherein there is no end.
> When thou sleepeth, guard for thyself thine own heart,
> For a man has no people,
> In the day of evil.
> I gave to the beggar,
> I nourished the orphan,
> I admitted the insignificant,
> As well as him who was of great account.
> But he who ate my food made insurrection,
> He to whom I gave my hand aroused fear therein."

> —from *A History of Egypt* by James A. Breasted

It would be a mistake to think of life in ancient Egypt as a continuous succession of sunny days during which time stood still. This is the impression one gets from studying the wall paintings in the tombs and the colossal statues in the temples. Pharaoh after Pharaoh went his way, each looking so much like the other that we cannot tell one of 3000 B.C. from one of 1000 B.C. But this was due to the rigid formalism of Egyptian art—a formalism that did not prevent the development of a much more subtle and individual style, as we know from examining the jewelry, ornaments, and pottery of the time. Life was not at all stiff, formal, and unchanging. Egyptians knew times of violent upheaval and change. They had their Classic Age, their Dark Ages, and their Renaissance. They loved life, because they knew it was so transitory and so uncertain. The Middle Kingdom lasted exactly 213 years, one month, and some days. Then came the Hyksos.

## The Hyksos

We don't know exactly who they were. Later Egyptian records speak of them as we speak of the Huns, "the Scourge of God." Certainly, they came out of the east, probably a bedouin tribe. But if Egypt fell before a bedouin tribe, things must have fallen pretty low indeed. After the Twelfth Dynasty died out, claimant after claimant seized the throne, while the land went back to ruin. Two hundred more years of this followed, with cities being burned, fields trampled, men, women, and children sold into slavery. Then the clouds lifted. Like a storm of locusts, the Hyksos moved on into Palestine. Of their empire almost no record remains.

It was a new Egypt which saw the light after the year 1600 B.C. Tremendous battles had been fought and the man who emerged as the savior of the country—his name was Ahmose I (Amasis)—was a mighty warrior-king. From now on, there would be no more petty nomarchs angling for power. This Pharaoh, by origin himself only a Theban princeling, would rule alone. An army of officials would take over Egypt to do his bidding. And behind him was the army, which would spread Egypt's frontiers to the ends of the known world.

## The Riddle of the Ka

To sample the flavor of this New Kingdom, we must leave the precincts of the Valley of the Kings and make a small excursion through the hills. It is best to go with a guide because the way over the eastern mountain is easily lost. After a climb of thirty or forty minutes, you stand on a height commanding an unforgettable view. Below you is the Nile Valley, green and sinuous, and at your feet, cut into the naked rust-red sandstone cliff, is the mortuary temple of Queen Hatshepsut. And here a bit of explanation is in order.

The Egyptians believed in the existence after death of a shadow-self called the *ka*. It cannot be described as the soul, for the soul was to be judged, but the *ka* was not judged. Instead, it accompanied the body wherever it went in this world and the next. Perhaps the German notion of the *Doppelgänger* or the Freudian concept of the Unconscious are as close as we can get to understanding the *ka* today. Whatever it was, it was hungry. Just as the body wanted to be fed when it was alive, the *ka* went in search of food for it when it was locked in its sarcophagus. So the family developed the habit of saving a bit of food from the table and slipping over to the tomb with it in the evening. The food was usually left in a funerary temple alongside the tomb.

Now this kindly custom created a gigantic problem for the Pharaohs. If the funerary temple was built alongside the tomb, it automatically gave away the location of the secret burial place. On the other hand, nobody could expect the *ka* to go very far from its body. How far could a *ka* walk? This knotty question must have puzzled the best priestly minds of Ancient Egypt for a long while. Evidently, they came up with the answer that an evening stroll of thirty or forty minutes out and back was not too much to expect of any self-respecting *ka*. Perhaps the *ka* needed the exercise. Anyhow, that was enough for the Pharaohs of the New Kingdom, who built their funerary temples on the *east* side of the mountain, directly opposite the spot where their bodies were to rest on the *west* side of the mountain.

## Queen Hatshepsut

The Temple of Queen Hatshepsut, begun just three generations after the expulsion of the Hyksos, is a brand-new kind of building—new in conception, new in beauty, new in size. In a series of three terraces it rises from the plain, the fronts of the terraces ranged with great colonnades, which when seen from the distance give an effect of grandeur equaling the Parthenon at Athens (which was not to be built for another one thousand years). Today Hatshepsut's temple stands stark and naked against the rugged mountainside, but when first built the terraces were

*The mortuary temple of Queen Hatshepsut, opposite Luxor.*

green with gardens and myrrh trees and on the walls were life-size pictures of the great expedition to Punt, "the home of the gods" (modern Somaliland?) to fetch the exotic trees, shrubs, and other ornaments of ivory, ebony, green gold, and cinnamon wood that were used to decorate the temple. The paintings, faded by exposure to the tropic sun for 3500 years, are still there, and as we muse among them we learn a story strange beyond anything Egypt has had to tell us yet.

Ahmose founded the Eighteenth Dynasty but its glory was not to be carried on by his male line. Rather, it fell to an upstart family, the Thutmosids, who married into the royal House. The ancient Egyptians always maintained that heredity was through the *female* line, although the husband held the power. Hence, to prevent the family from being broken up, it was habitual for brothers and sisters to marry, so that the blood should be kept pure. This was all the more important in the house of the Pharaoh, in order to maintain the fiction that he was descended from the sun-god. Consanguinity in marriage held no horror for the people of Ancient Egypt, and many Pharaohs married, beside their sisters, their nieces, aunts, and cousins as well. This makes a complete hash of any family tree, and it is often next to impossible to know whether the reigning monarch is husband, son, brother, or father of the true heiress!

Sometimes, however, when no son survived, it was necessary for the heiress to marry outside the family. This happened in the case of Thutmose I. His claim to the throne rested entirely on his marriage to the princess of the old House, also named Ahmose. The reign of Thutmose was marked by great victories, as he reestablished the rule of Egypt over the whole of the known world from the third cataract of the Nile in the south to the great bend of the Euphrates in the north.

But Thutmose's position was at once weakened by the death of his wife. Suddenly, he had no claim to the throne in his own right. He was not of the blood of the sun-god. The only surviving daughter of the House was Hatshepsut, sometimes called "the first woman in history." For a time Thutmose got by, by proclaiming Hatshepsut his successor. But obviously this wouldn't do, and she became co-regent. And then, suddenly, during a dramatic moment in the Temple of Amon at Thebes, while the elderly Thutmose was actually burning incense to the gods, he was overthrown by the god himself.

The priests, according to their custom, bore the statue of the god around the colonnade, as if he were looking for someone, and he finally stopped before a young prince, son of Thutmose I by a concubine, and married to Hatshepsut. The prince, whose name was also Thutmose, prostrated himself. And then the awful thing happened. The god nodded toward the youth, thereby clearly recognizing him as Pharaoh. Innumerable (probably paid) witnesses claimed they saw it with their own eyes. The incident has been recorded on the walls of the temple for us to see to this day.

The younger Thutmose overthrew his own father and reigned in his place. His claim was entirely through his wife and half sister, Hatshepsut, just as his father's claim had been through Ahmose. And if Hatshepsut had been a quiet, peaceable woman like all the other heiresses in the previous two thousand years of Egyptian history, that would have been the end of it. But she wasn't. She had been named to the succession, and she had worn the royal cobra on her forehead as co-regent with her father. Now *she* would be Pharaoh.

Never before had a woman reigned in Egypt. It is a testimony to the extraordinary personality of this woman that she pulled it off. How she did it, we don't know. But suddenly there she is in the pictures and monuments, the cobra on her forehead, the crown of Upper and Lower Egypt on her head, the beard on her chin—yes, Pharaoh must have a beard, even if he—or rather, she—is a woman.

How her husband, Thutmose, felt about all this, we don't know, but

*A possible likeness of Queen Hatshepsut? From Hatshepsut's mortuary temple.*

we can guess. What good was the support of the priests of Amon (which must have cost him a pretty penny!) if a mere woman could countermand the nod of the god? But Hatshepsut even got around the god, too. On the walls of her temple she had sculptured a series of reliefs showing her miraculous birth, her mother, Ahmose, visited by the god, who names Hatshepsut *his* daughter, herself at birth *as a boy*. She is called "a female Horus" and the word "Majesty" appears for the first time in the feminine gender.

But if you look closer at these reliefs, you see the marks of a chisel, obliterating a certain royal cartouche (symbol) over and over again. It is the cartouche of Hatshepsut. For Thutmose could not sit idly by while all this happened. He had his party ready in the wings. Even old Thutmose I was still alive, grinding his teeth at this female impostor. Father and son made common cause and Hatshepsut was cast aside. Every where on her favorite temple her name was erased. New wall paintings appeared, showing the elder Thutmose once again in command, marching at the head of his army into Asia, and receiving the tribute of the vanquished. Then the old man died.

Once again, Hatshepsut asserted herself. Soon the woman with the beard is seen again in more murals, restoring public works that had suffered from the reign of the Hyksos, erecting mighty temples, and six of the highest obelisks the world had ever seen—one of them still stands across the river at Luxor, 97½ feet high, and made of a single block. Hatshepsut was a devotee of peace and exerted herself for fifteen years in beautifying the country. Speaking directly to us across 3,500 years, she says on her inscriptions:

> You who after long years shall see these monuments, who shall speak of what I have done, you will say, "we do not know, we do not know how they can have made a whole mountain of gold as if it were an ordinary task." . . . To gild these I have given gold measured by the bushel, as though it were sacks of grain. And when My Majesty had said the amount, it was more than the whole of the Two Lands had ever seen . . . when you shall hear this, do not say that it is an idle boast, but say—"how like her this was, worthy of her father Amon!"

> *—A History of Egypt*

*On the walls of the mortuary temple of Queen Hatshepsut, Thutmose III is shown before the gods of the Underworld.*

Yes, Your Majesty, we say it, as we walk around your mortuary temple in the red limestone cliffs opposite Luxor. But we look in vain for your name, or your face. We shall never know how you looked, what beauty was yours, for you must have had a great beauty and an unspeakable charm behind that beard of yours to turn Egypt on its head for fifteen years! But alas, all this has been erased. You must have expected it. Thutmose was your enemy. Yet, woman that you were, you let him live, just as you let your earthly father, the elder Thutmose, live. There your woman's heart betrayed you.

Suddenly Hatshepsut is no more. It is the name of Thutmose III that appears on all the monuments—back on the warpath in Asia, winning victories over the black Nubians and the aquiline Assyrians, leading his captives home in chains. . . . Even on the walls of the mortuary temple it is Thutmose who is painted in place of Hatshepsut, offering incense to the god Amon. Thutmose, Thutmose, Thutmose—everywhere in Egypt and beyond the name is going up on boundary stelae, on obelisks, and especially on the great temple of Karnak on the west bank of the Nile at Luxor.

You must now leave the precincts of the limestone cliffs, and board the riverboat again to return to the other side, for it is here that history is now being written. But, looking back at the fading outline of Hatshepsut's temple, you cannot help thinking of the valiant struggle of a single woman against all the colossal weight of tradition. A foolish struggle, perhaps. Egypt was not ready for a woman at the helm, nor was it what the time needed.

This was the first great period of Empire. There were enemies pressing on all the frontiers, and while Hatshepsut sent expeditions to Punt, to gather myrrh trees, she should have been sending expeditions to Asia and Nubia to protect the imperial possessions. No wonder Thutmose ground his teeth in silence as he saw the empire wasting away while the Court played at gardening, like Marie Antoinette in the Trianon. Hatshepsut had to go. Whether Thutmose poisoned her or she died of a broken heart (for evidently she loved him), we shall never know.

The sun sets behind the Theban hills in the west and you return to your hotel in Luxor. Perhaps your window opens on the waterfront and you can hear the song of the boatman in the dark. The thought haunts you that the Queen Pharaoh crossed the river, too, after visiting her temple and walking among the myrrh trees in the evening—a woman advanced before her time.

# The Empire

## Karnak

Just a few miles to the north of Luxor stands Karnak, the temple city. Your arabiyah (horse and buggy) will take you there in a few minutes and put you down in the untidy square, crowded with fallen blocks of stone, hawkers of "antiquities," and children from the neighboring village in the palm grove in search of *baksheesh*. Before you lies the Avenue of Sphynxes, which leads to a great boxlike structure, roofless, but filled with a forest of columns, 134 altogether, seventy feet tall and at least ten feet in diameter. You are in the Great Temple of Amon.

Look around you and you will see not only one of the most gigantic ruins left by any civilization, but also an astounding record of achievement. For this famous hall, the courtyards, the temple area itself farther on, all shout at you with one voice: Long live the Empire! The great Temple of Amon, built in honor of the god, is in reality a showplace for the boasting of the Empire builders. The columns are covered with boastful statements; so are all the obelisks in the courtyards. The pylons, or gateways, to each of the temple areas all tell the story of achievement. "Look at what I did," they challenge you. And, indeed, the achievement is very great.

Start with the pylon of Thutmose III, Hatshepsut's husband (another brother, known as Thutmose II, had reigned briefly during the struggle for power) at the eastern end of the temple complex. Here you may see

*Gateway built by the Greek Pharaohs, the Ptolemies (332–30 B.C.) at Karnak.*

55

the list of 119 towns captured by the Pharaoh on his early campaigns, while of his later victories there is a list of 248 towns that submitted to him. People in ancient times had only to look at the obelisks to read of the glory of "Thutmose, who crossed the great 'Bend of Naharin' [the Euphrates] with might and with victory at the head of his army," All his obelisks have disappeared from Egypt, but one can be seen today in Central Park in New York and another beside the Thames in London.

## An Era of Splendor

If you could stand on the steps of the Temple of Amon and turn back the clock to the year 1459 B.C., the year of Thutmose's seventeenth and last campaign, you would see a new Egypt. In the gardens of the temple, stretching down to the river, grow strange new plants and trees from Syria and Palestine; animals unknown to the hunter of the Nile Valley wander among the trees. Tied up at the wharves along the riverbank are Phoenician galleys, unloading cargoes of gold, and silver workmanship from Tyre, Cyprus, Crete, and the Aegean Isles. Then there are the human cargoes—Asiatics with long, matted beards (held in contempt in Egypt), their arms pinioned behind them or manacled in front. The crowd laughs and gibes at the poor wretches who are sold into slavery.

This was an imperial Egypt, and Thebes had become a cosmopolitan city composed of splendid houses and villas, each with forecourt and a garden that gave onto the river. The people who lived in these houses were luxury-loving sophisticates who drove out in chariots of silver and gold, wearing full-length pleated robes, elaborately curled wigs, and oriental pointed shoes.

All this was nothing, of course, compared to the splendor of the palace of the Pharaoh himself. Of this nothing remains. The palaces, like the houses of the time, were built of wood; only the temples were built of stone. But the contents of museums around the world give us some idea of what the palace was like inside. Dishes, cups, vessels of gold and silver, covered with figures of men and animals, plants and flowers, shone on the royal table. The walls were hung with tapestry, in colors and designs equal or superior to anything else created since. Floors and walls were covered with glazed tiles that were decorated with designs in gold leaf.

56

*An example of Egyptian splendor during the Empire period. Tutenkhamon's throne shows the Pharaoh himself with his queen under the rays of the sun god.*

In the gardens at Luxor, where you walk between the temple and the town, there was a large lake, about a mile long and a thousand feet wide, and here the Pharaoh sailed with his queen in a royal barge, accompanied by an orchestra of harps tall as a man, lyres just introduced from Asia, and pipes. Another of Thutmose's favorite pastimes was the hunt. When he received word that a herd of wild cattle was roaming the Delta, he would sail north all night and reach the herd by morning. Troops and villagers then drove the cattle into a large enclosure. Standing up in his chariot, the Pharaoh slew fifty-six beasts in a single day.

There is something startlingly new and modern about all this. The Pharaoh, formerly a remote, godlike figure, is now seen and heard and talked about as a human being. Thutmose made the throne of the Pharaohs a subject for popular acclaim. But with acclaim comes dissent. Egypt was growing up. Questions were being asked about the divine origin of the Pharaoh. Everyone knew he formerly had been an obscure prince, not of the royal blood, and that the priests of Amon had made him into a Pharaoh. Questions were also asked about the priesthood and about the multitude of gods that preyed on the souls and purses of the people. Visiting wise men out of Asia questioned all these things and even mentioned a new belief among the Hebrews, an obscure Semitic tribe—a belief in one God.

Thutmose went to his rest in the Theban hills untroubled about the future. His heirs, like him, continued to enjoy life and to plunge deep into the affluence that Egypt's Empire period poured into their laps. More temples went up, the statues grew larger and larger, like the two colossi across the river built by Amenhotep III in his own honor, the largest statues in the world. More and more money was being spent

*The colossi of Memnon are representations of Amenhotep III. They were damaged by an earthquake in ancient times.*

on elaborate tombs in the Valley of the Kings, just as if no dissent existed. But the dissenters would not be silenced, and, as often happens, they found a spokesman right in the royal family itself.

## Ikhnaton

Amenhotep's son, young Amenhotep IV, was a dreamer. He read a great deal and probably thought too much. His mother, Queen Tiy, and his wife, Nefretete (Nefertiti), both very strong-minded women, had great influence over him. In fact, the very idea he came to adopt may have been their idea, picked up from the host of itinerant intellectuals who converged on Thebes. He also seems to have had all the Freudian symptoms of hostility toward his father. When the pleasure-loving Amenhotep III died in the year 1375 B.C., his son embarked on a new kind of reign.

He changed his name. No longer would he bear the name of his father's god Amon. Instead he named himself Ikhnaton (Akhenaton), which means "Spirit of Light," because he worshiped the sun, "Aton," as the only god. What's more, he sent thousands of men to work all over the Empire, with picks and chisels, hacking out the name of Amon wherever it appeared. And since the word "Amon" appeared in his father's name, that too had to be effaced everywhere. The Great Temple of Amon at Thebes was closed, its priesthood disbanded. The old religion was proscribed, its rites abolished. No longer would people embalm their dead and lavish their earnings on their tombs. Ikhnaton turned his back on the great city of Thebes with its temples and palaces and vast necropolis across the river. He summoned his royal barge, and going aboard with his mother and wife, he sailed away to found a new city, dedicated to a higher and better way of life.

If you would follow him today—and, surely, in a breathtaking adventure like this you will want to do so—you must take a train north from Luxor about three hundred miles to the modern village of Tell-el-Amarna. Actually, the railway station is Mallawi on the west bank of the Nile. It is not easy to get to the site of Akhetaton, the Abode of Light, as Ikhnaton called his city. You are far off the tourist track here. You'll have to take a car—probably an old, jolting Ford—from the station down to the river and then hire a felucca, for the site of Akhetaton is on the other side.

A felucca is a three-masted Nile boat with triangular sails and oars. It negotiates the strong current easily, and in a few minutes you are on the eastern bank. Perhaps your guide has had the forethought to bring donkeys along in the felucca. Otherwise, you will need to hire them now, for the journey is several miles from the landing under a burning sun. Riding a donkey, it is quite impossible to look dignified, but if you simply relax you will find that no one regards you as in the least foolish-looking. The children who rush after you screaming are simply asking for *baksheesh* (begging for money) as you amble through the mud-brick villages, beside the green bean fields and over the endless, sky-reflecting canals.

Soon you leave the palm grove and emerge onto a desert plain that lies between the eastern cliffs and the river Nile. This is the site chosen by the dreamer king for his new capital. Do not expect to see great temples and monuments here. Mounds, ditches, lines of low mud-brick walls, boundary stones—that is all that remains of the city of Akhetaton—that and the tombs of its founder in the cliff beyond.

When Iknhaton laid out his dream city, thousands of workmen were engaged in laying out its streets, parks, villas, and palaces for the Pharaoh and his court. And in the center of it all was the Temple of Aton. Who was Aton? Nobody really knew. Aton is the sun, the giver of light and life. A new priesthood arose, who daily chanted a hymn of praise to the sun, written by the Pharaoh himself:

> "Thy dawning is beautiful in the horizon of heaven,
> O living Aton, Beginning of Life!
> When thou risest in the eastern horizon of heaven,
> Thou fillest every land with thy beauty;
> For thou art beautiful, great, glittering, high over the earth;
> Thy rays, they encompass the lands, even all thou hath made.
> Thou art Re, and thou hast carried them all away captive,
> Thou bindest them by thy love.
> Though thou art afar, thy rays are on earth
> Though thou art on high, thy footprints are the day."
>
> —*A History of Egypt*

*The head of Queen Nefretete and her husband Ikhnaton, the heretic Pharaoh who
founded a new monotheistic religion in Ancient Egypt which did not outlive him.*

In this dream city, cut off from all the realities of life, worshiping
the god of his own invention, the dreamer king and his wife lived an
ideal life for seventeen years. We can glimpse what it was like in the
paintings on the walls of the tombs along the eastern cliffs. Banished from
these walls are all the hideous demons of the afterlife which populated
the tombs of the past. Here is only beauty and truth, the rays of the sun
reaching down, each ray ending in a human hand to help humanity.
And here you see the Pharaoh and his wife, Nefretete, appearing among
the people simply and naturally like ordinary citizens. In some scenes
Ikhnaton, wraps his arm about Nefretete's waist, in another he eats a
chicken leg with her, seated on his throne. For Ikhnaton, as it was for

61

Keats three thousand years later, "Beauty is truth, truth beauty—that is all ye know on earth, and all ye need to know."

Meanwhile, what was happening outside the walls of the dream city? Buried in the sand at Tell-el-Amarna, the correspondence of the Pharaoh has come to light. Here are the letters of his commanders and governors in the distant parts of the Empire. All are calling for help, as town after town is seized by the enemies of Egypt.

"For twenty years," writes one, "we have been sending to our lord the King but there has come to us not a word, no not one."

Another laments, "The whole land of my lord the King is going to ruin."

And in Egypt itself, unemployment, hunger, and revolt stalked the land. Temples were closed, the priests disbanded, the embalmers, the painters, the makers of tomb furnishings out of work . . . everywhere there was dissatisfaction. The people were lost without their old,

*The mask of King Tutenkhamon is made of pure gold and weighs over 900 pounds. On the Pharaoh's forehead are the serpent goddess of the North and the vulture goddess of the South.*

cherished beliefs in Osiris, Isis, and Horus, their protectors in the here-after. They did not understand Aton. There was no one to explain it to them. The revolution of Ikhnaton had been a closed revolution, for the benefit of a small coterie of intellectuals. It had no roots.

Shortly after his death, the counterrevolution broke out. His successor, Tutenkhaton (Tut-ankh-aton), returned to Thebes and made his peace with Amon, changing his name to Tutenkh*amon* (Tut-ankh-amon). And the day of vengeance had come. With grim fury, the priests of Amon visited the city of Akhetaton and leveled it to the ground. Every-where they chiseled out the hated name of Ikhnaton, replacing it for the historical record with the words "the criminal of Akhetaton." The old struggle for power, the wars between Osiris and Set, were renewed. Pharaoh after Pharaoh fought his way to the throne and was in turn overthrown. So ended the Eighteenth Dynasty in blood and chaos.

We shudder at the violence of Pharaonic times, forgetting that the rhythm of peace and war, order and chaos is much more prolonged than in any subsequent period of history. Periods of calm in Ancient Egypt lasted for hundreds of years, interspersed by periods of break-down. But all the while, perhaps even during the most intense civil strife, the shaduf endlessly lifts the waters of the Nile, the scribes and the potters and the embalmers continue their work, the well-to-do ladies sit under their parasols applying cosmetics to their eyes, the hunters go out at dawn to catch ducks in the marshes with their boomerangs, the slaves sweat as they pull the great blocks of granite by rope over the sands for the newest monument. Ancient Egypt was probably the calmest and most even-tempered period in human history.

## Rameses the Great

As you turn your back on Tell-el-Amarna and the bright tomb pictures of the lost dream city, you will have to travel northward to find the traces of the next great age in Egypt. Past modern Cairo, the Nile divides into many branches seeking the sea. This is the Delta, as rich in ancient times as it is today. In this broad plain, among the watercourses, stood the famous towns of Lower Egypt—Heliopolis (the On of the Bible), Tanis (the biblical Zoan), and Per Ramese. The roads today are dusty and

*The Temple of Karnak seems eternal. Carvings on its pillars celebrate the victories of Rameses II about 1300 B.C.*

teeming with village life, and as you drive along them you will pass on your way many a flattened column or fallen colossus among the salt-sands and marshes of this coastal land.

On a tongue of land between the sea and Lake Manzala, near the modern city of Port Said, you may ask for the town of Qantir. The citizens of Qantir may not know it themselves, but they are living on the ruins of one of the greatest cities of antiquity—Per Ramese, built by the Pharaohs of the Nineteenth Dynasty. Little now remains to see, unless you find a knowledgeable guide who can identify the crumbling mud-brick ruins of a palace and some houses—all that is left of the treasure-house residence of Rameses II.

Yet Per Ramese has been described by a poet of its time as "beauteous with balconies and dazzling halls of lapis lazuli and turquoise, the places

64

where the chariotry is marshaled and the infantry assembles and where the warships come to anchorage when the tribute is brought." On the Pharaoh's table were the latest rarities and delicacies from Cyprus. The chariots came from Palestine and Syria, the horses in its stables were from Babylon. All this reflected the renewed power and vigor of the Empire under Rameses the Great.

The Nineteenth Dynasty, founded like many another by an ordinary official who obtained the support of the priests of Amon, became the most glorious in Egyptian history. It lasted for 142 years and, taken together with the opening years of the Twentieth Dynasty, it marks the climax of Egypt's greatness. Much of this was the work of one man, Rameses II. Everywhere we go in the Nile Valley we see the overwhelming evidence of his accomplishment.

In the Theban hills is the great Rameseum, or mortuary temple, on which the Pharaoh lavished his wealth for six decades. Today it is nothing but a vast heap of ruins, yet it is worth visiting. You will stand with awe before the recumbent statue of Rameses, 56 feet tall, shoulders 23 feet broad, index finger 3 feet long. Hewn out of a single piece of granite, it lies broken in three places. Standing in the Rameseum before the fallen colossus, you cannot help but repeat after Shelley:

> "My name is Ozymandias, king of kings:
> Look on my works, ye Mighty, and despair!"
> Nothing beside remains. Round the decay
> Of that colossal wreck, boundless and bare
> The lone and level sands stretch far away."
> —from "Ozymandias" [1817]

Across the river, at Thebes, the Great Hall of Karnak displays on its walls the endless record of Rameses' conquest and victory. When you stand here and gaze down the splendid aisles, roofed by hundred-ton architraves; when you consider that this hall alone could contain the largest cathedral in the world with room to spare; when you observe the colossal gate over which once lay a lintel block weighing 150 tons— you cannot but admire the grandeur of this man and his civilization.

Far upstream at Abu Simbel, on the Nubian frontier, which you can reach in a hydrofoil, or flying boat, from Aswan, the features of Rameses

II ("the wrinkled lip, the sneer of cold command") outside his temple will still overawe you. The rescue of these monuments from the rising waters of Lake Nasser behind the new Aswan High Dam is a story in itself. When Abu Simbel was first threatened by the new project, it seemed doubtful that anything could be done to rescue the two temples there. Then an international consortium of construction companies (Joint Venture Abu Simbel), with funds provided by Egypt, the United States, and UNESCO, went to work. The task involved engineers from five countries and approximately four thousand man-years of work. The Great Temple, faced by four colossal statues of Rameses, was cut into the living rock and so oriented that twice a year the sun would strike into the heart of the sanctuary and illuminate the features of the god Re. Since the waters of

*The Temple of Abu Simbel in Nubia before it was moved due to the flooding of the Nile.*

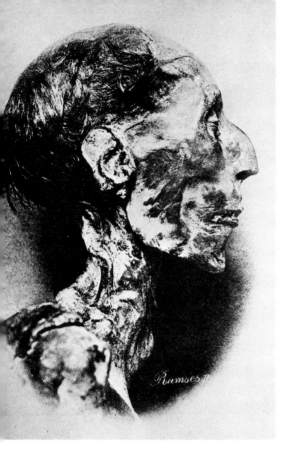

*The mummy of Rameses II, who died in his nineties.*

the Nile would flood this area, the facades of the temples, the colossi, and the interior paintings all had to be dismantled and lifted to a site two hundred feet higher. Furthermore, a new man-made mountain had to be built to house the original temples—supported by a concrete structure more ambitious than any built before—a truly "Ramesian" achievement! Rameses has been rescued at a cost of $36 million. But the fellah, singing beside his shaduf in the field, earns perhaps no more than $36 a year. Who will rescue him?

In all the monuments there is one theme—the greatness of Egypt, its eternal story, its unconquerable might. Usually when a people or a nation comes to believe it can never die, it is very close to death. There is something boastful about these monuments that sets your teeth on edge. This might be said also about Rameses. He talked too much about his victories. Like Egypt, his time had come and he didn't know it.

When he lay dying in his sumptuous palace at Per Ramese, in 1225 B.C., incredibly old (he was over ninety), surrounded by a family of over a hundred sons and at least fifty daughters and by generals and ministers and secretaries who brought him only soothing news, he believed himself *the* ruler of the known world. He did not know that at that very moment the barbarian Sea Peoples of Sardinia, Sicily, and the Aegean were encamped under his very walls. No one had dared to tell him.

## The Decline of Ancient Egypt

The rest of the story of Ancient Egypt is one of endless rot and decay. The world outside was now in turmoil, and new nations, new ideas, of which the Pharaohs had never heard, were being born. The Greeks penetrated to all the lands of the Mediterranean. Democracy was born at Athens. Philosophy and science sprang up in Ionia. The Hittites developed the battle-ax and the heavy chariot, neither of which the Egyptians had. Great new empires, Assyria and Persia, arose in the east.

Egypt failed to rise to any of these new challenges. Because her people had been among the first to establish a workable human society, they never considered for a moment any new thoughts. While men in Athens were grappling with new problems like universal suffrage, the ideal republic, the curvature of the earth, the priests of Amon were still selling Egyptians the Book of the Dead, telling them how to avoid the forty-two perils of the Underworld.

One after another, foreign states took over Egypt, establishing their own puppets there. In 525 B.C., the Persian Cambyses founded his own dynasty; in 332 B.C. came the Greek conquest under Alexander the Great, who established a line of Greek Pharaohs, the Ptolemies. The famous Cleopatra was one of these. A faint and flickering glamour hangs over these late Pharaohs, but they are all impostors, dressed up in the trappings of Khufu, Thutmose, and Rameses. Egypt—the Egypt of the Old Kingdom, the Middle Kingdom, and the Empire—was dead.

Dead? In a political sense, yes. But in a purely human sense, Ancient

Egypt has never died. The Egyptian people are probably the most homogeneous people in the world. The blood of the fellahin is pure Ancient Egyptian. The houses of mud bricks, the shaduf squeaking in the field, the charms, amulets, scarabs sold by the local sorcerer (druggist) in any village—all these things date from Pharaonic times.

To people like this, life is eternal; they have lived too long and seen too much to be attracted by false promises of progress; they do not care for war and politics or great causes. Thought to be ignorant and backward by Western standards, they regard Westerners as both boorish and naïve. They are often considered by foreigners to be dishonest and immoral; but this is only due to their cunning, and in the remote villages, the people are probably among the most honest and moral in the world. Historians ignore them because they neither complain about their lot nor mount any rebellion against the established powers of the world.

We lose sight of the simple people of Egypt for many centuries now, as other events fill the history books, but we can be sure they are always there, singing in the fields by day, or on the rooftops in the cool of the evening, and pursuing the truly eternal destiny of man—the survival of the human family. When we glimpse them again, a new age has dawned.

# Interlude
# A Walk Along the Corniche
# in Alexandria

To walk along the Corniche at Alexandria is one of the splendid moments of a lifetime. To the north lies the sea, blue-green as only the Mediterranean can be, washing long white breakers on the wide sands of the beach. And what a beach! There seems to be no end to the rows of colored umbrellas, the candy-striped bathing houses, the throngs of people, soaking up the sun or frolicking in the waves.

And to the south, on the landward side, the avenue is lined, mile after mile, by the high, white house fronts of the luxury villas and hotels. Behind these ornate facades are the streets of the European quarter. Alexandria is rather European in character, and you come here not to see Egypt but to see that fascinating, exotic flower—a hybrid culture.

In the eastern harbor, behind the great breakwater, the fishing fleets are drawn up, unloading their catch, although local gossip will tell you that "times are not what they used to be"; the building of the Aswan High Dam has stopped the annual flood, and the mackerel no longer ascend the river to spawn. Alas! There seems to be no good that does not harm someone at the same time!

Beyond the East Harbour rises the Quait Bai Fort. It is worth a visit.

*Known as the Queen of the Mediterranean, Alexandria is one of the loveliest summer resorts of Egypt. The famous Corniche Drive, seen in the background, runs all along the coast.*

*The principal mosque in Alexandria. East and West, old and new blend harmoniously as a gay Egyptian crowd gathers in the square.*

Just think—you are standing on the site of the famous lighthouse on Pharos, which was built by Ptolemy II in 280 B.C. and destroyed by an earthquake only in the fourteenth century.

In those days, according to the historian Edward Gibbon, Alexandria consisted of 4,000 palaces, 400 theaters, and a population of 300,000 free inhabitants as well as a multitude of slaves. The greatest scientists and artists in the world lived here and taught at the Academy. But it was not an Egyptian city then; it was part of one or another of the world empires that flourished in antiquity: first, the Macedonian Empire of Alexander the Great (who founded the city); next the Roman Empire; then the Byzantine Empire. The people who walked these streets were

Greeks, Romans, Phoenicians, or Jews—but rarely Egyptians, just as today you see more Western styles, you hear more French or Italian or even Russian spoken here than anywhere else in Egypt.

Plunge into one of these French-style streets leading away from the seafront and you will come in a moment to the Graeco-Roman Museum, off Fuad I Avenue. Here, in these walls is almost all that remains of that vanished world of international civilization that ruled Egypt for a thousand years, from the conquest of Alexander (332 B.C.) to the coming of Islam (A.D. 640). That thought alone may make you shiver a little. One thousand years of grandeur, the work of the best minds, the library of 700,000 books—and all that is left is in a few cases!

One of the objects that may stir a memory is the colossal green granite head of Antony, friend of Caesar and lover of Cleopatra, who met his death here in Egypt. Who has not been fascinated by this famous love affair? Cleopatra, heir to the Ptolemies, a Pharaoh at eighteen (the first woman Pharaoh after Hatshepsut), was highly educated in sciences and languages, and so beautiful that she enslaved all the men who were sent against her. First the Roman general Pompey arrived at the head of

*The University of Alexandria.*

an army. He surrendered to her charms. Then, after his murder, came Caesar, who also fell for her. Caesar, too, died by the knife. Then came Antony. Ah, says legend, but she loved Antony, and when Rome sent yet another general to arrest her lover, Cleopatra chose to die with him. Today, when we think of Egypt, we often think first of Cleopatra and the serpent she took to her bosom: "I am dying, Egypt, dying!" A splendid woman—but she wasn't a true Egyptian.

Even today, as you continue now along Fuad I Avenue, with its smart shops and showrooms, and you jostle with the well-to-do throng on the sidewalk, you feel you are in a European city. For the city looks westward not eastward. When you come at last to the Western Harbour, a jungle of shipping meets your eye—ships from every quarter of the globe, ranged along two and a half miles of quays, for the greater part of Egypt's export and import trade passes through this port.

*The port of Alexandria is one of the busiest harbors in the Mediterranean.*

And yet, all this activity can be deceptive, too. Stop for a moment and look in the antique stores that cluster around this neighborhood. In a moment, a light switches on, a shop door opens, and a Greek merchant invites you to step in. Quickly, he moves about the interior, turning on the lights in the showcases. What are you interested in? Egyptian antiquities, scarabs, mummy ornaments? Victorian knick-knacks, hand-carved mirrors, faded love lockets? Or what about the real prize in Alexandria—a few alexandrite stones?

In an instant he unrolls a velvet cloth on the counter and shakes out on it a hail of small and medium-size stones, smooth and flat on one side and bevel-edged on the other. They glitter a deep mauve. Then he switches on another light. The stones turn green and glow phosphorescently.

It is best to buy them without settings, says the Greek, because this government (did he add some expletives under his breath?) charges the merchant so much more than the world price for gold that it spoils a good bargain. Business is not so good these days, he admits. His customers are all Western, and the government (that guttural word slips in again) doesn't care about the Western trade any more. Everything goes to "the war." In the end, either because you sympathize with the merchant, or because you admire the stone, you make a small purchase and leave the store. Sadly, he puts the lights out after you, to save on the electricity bill, presumably, and waits for the next customer in darkness.

Any day, you may stop at one of the Coptic churches as the crowd is going in to Mass. If you are lucky you may even persuade the priest, or one of the congregation, to show you around. The church is usually rectangular, with the sanctuary at the far end entirely screened off by three iconostases, or partitions, with a door and two windows facing the altar. These partitions are decorated with paintings, sometimes inlaid with ivory and surmounted with icons of Christ, the Holy Virgin, the apostles and saints.

Yet there is something much older than Christianity here. Perhaps it is the pillars, which are apt to be taken from old Egyptian temples,

*The flower clock at Alexandria.*

hieroglyphics and all (but consecrated with crosses). Perhaps it is the ritual music of the choir, accompanied by cymbals, triangles, handbells, and flutes—all directly descended from the temple music of the Pharaohs. Or perhaps it is the congregation, which seems of poor but ancient lineage. Only about 7 percent of the population are now Copts, your guide will tell you. But then he will recall, almost as though he could remember it himself, the great era when all Egypt was Coptic.

This was in the early days of Christianity. By tradition, it was here that St. Mark preached to the Egyptians, and Alexandria became the center of the new faith. Under the Romans, there was severe persecution of the Christians (the Copts date their calendar from the persecution of A.D. 284), but the Coptic Church endured. Later, however, it seceded from the Orthodox and Western Churches on the Monophysite controversy. At the Council of Chalcedon in A.D. 451, the Copts refused to assent to the doctrine of the two natures of Christ, human and divine. They accepted only the divine. This was the beginning of the national Egyptian church.

Undoubtedly your Coptic guide will impress upon you his people's greatest pride—the purity of blood. "We are the only true Egyptians," say the Copts (often, however, in lowered voices). "We alone have kept the blood untainted by marriage with foreigners" (meaning the Arabs). "But," your guide will hasten to add, "we are a hundred percent behind our President. We are all for the war against Israel and we pray to God for victory soon!"

Such are the currents and cross-currents that ruffle the surface in this pearl among cities in the eastern Mediterranean, a city with a glorious past, an uncertain present, and a future that depends on the turn of the weather vane. Today, Alexandria looks wistfully westward. But the wind is blowing hard east.

# The Coming of Islam

## Ibn Tulun

You are in the cloisters of the Ibn Tulun Mosque in Old Cairo. Outside, the cacophony of motor horns, the braying of donkeys, the clucking of fowl and geese as they scurry away from the wheels of passing cars, the endless hammering on brass by the metalworkers in their doorways, the quarreling of the merchants, the screams of children playing on the street—all fade away behind these massive brick walls.

Inside, all is calm, order, peace. Around the great open central courtyard, 300 feet square, filled with sunlight, run the colonnades, a forest of tall, massive pillars, arching overhead, filled with shadow. On three sides, the colonnades are two aisles deep; on the southeast side—facing Mecca—is a four-aisled sanctuary, hung with lamps on long chains.

At an outside corner of the building rises a minaret of curious design with a spiral outside stairway. From the platform at the top the muezzin utters his strident call to prayer five times a day: *"Allah-hu-Akbar.* There is no god but God, and Muhammad is His prophet. . . ."

In the center of the courtyard stands an octagonal building under a pointed dome. This contains the running water for ablutions. At the hour of prayer, the faithful pass through this ablution chamber, wetting their hands, feet, and face, as a preparation for meeting God. The prayers are led by an imam, or priest, who mounts the pulpit in the southeastern colonnade and recites the Koran. The crowds spread their prayer mats before them and stand, kneel, and prostrate themselves, always

*The Mosque of Ibn Tulun, showing the central courtyard and the minaret from which the muezzin calls the faithful to prayer. This is the oldest mosque in Egypt, dating from the ninth century.*

*Arches in the Mosque of Ibn Tulun. The Arabs first used the pointed arch, which was later introduced into Europe as the hallmark of Gothic architecture.*

facing Mecca. In a few moments, all is over and everyone disperses, gossiping. You have the mosque to yourself again.

This is the most ancient mosque in Egypt, built by the fierce, fanatical Ahmad ibn Tulun in the ninth century. What today seems very old, almost as old as Egypt itself, was then very new, brash, and bold. Ibn Tulun belonged to the race of conquering Arabs who swarmed over Egypt in the seventh century. Like the wind of God, they came out of the desert, scattering the remnants of ancient empires before them, even as leaves in autumn.

But Ibn Tulun was the first who settled down to found his own city and dynasty. He called the city Fostat, which means "armed camp," later to become Cairo. Egyptian laborers were requisitioned for the new palaces, markets, and the mosque, just as they had labored for the Pharaohs of old. But this mosque was a new kind of building for them. Modeled on the old *kaaba* (place of prayer) in Mecca, it was like a desert oasis, rather than a god-haunted sanctuary—the columns around the courtyard resembling a palm grove, and the central portion, being open, devoid of mystery. This was a new kind of religion—plain, dogmatic, earth-bound.

And the men who brought it were new to Egypt too—men of the

desert with aquiline features. Of course, Egypt had seen so many foreigners by this time that it made little difference what they were like. They would soon settle down and become Egyptians, too. So said the wise old men of the Nile, nodding their heads around their village fires.

The Arabs were not just like other conquerors—the Persians, the Greeks, the Romans. These new rulers had a fanatic belief in their new faith, which they called Islam. Proclaimed by Muhammad in the year A.D. 622 (called the year 1 by the Moslems), Islam spread over most of the known world in one century, from the borders of China in the east to the heart of France in the west. But they were a primitive people, who had everything to learn from their subject peoples. And in Egypt their first schism began.

Ibn Tulun came to Egypt as lieutenant to the caliph in faraway Baghdad. But he soon made himself independent. This was the turning point. It marked the emergence in the Nile Valley of a sovereign state that maintained itself throughout the Middle Ages. For the first time since the Pharaohs, Egypt was an independent nation, albeit with foreign masters. And as in the days of Thutmose III, Ibn Tulun carved out an empire in Syria that was to last many centuries.

Little remains of the Tulunid glory, for the old conqueror was not blessed in his family. His sons and grandsons were pleasure seekers who had no taste for a warrior's life and preferred to pass their time in palace intrigues. One of them, the infamous Khumarawayh, even built himself a pool of quicksilver in his palace. Leather cushions filled with air floated on the surface of this pool, fastened to the side by silken cords. There the dynast used to loll, rocking himself agreeably to sleep, while the armies of the caliph of Baghdad stormed at the gates. Traces of the quicksilver have actually been found at the site.

Only the grim old mosque remains. As you leave, cast a thought of pity for the desert warrior whose hard-won kingdom was wasted by his sons. He was not the last to find that sudden affluence breeds weakness and opens a gap between the generations. But his idea—an independent Islam on the Nile—was to bear fruit nonetheless.

What this idea needed was a new prophet who would provide a doctrinal argument for the break with Baghdad. This man was actually at work spreading his teaching across North Africa at this time. His name was al-Shii—hence the heresy came by the name of Shiism.

His candidate for the throne in the North African Kingdom of Tunisia was a certain Said Ibn Husayn, who soon swept all before him. From Morocco to the confines of Egypt, the soldiers of the new faith carried fire and sword, even harrying the coasts of Europe and carrying off slaves. (Thus they became known as the Barbary pirates.) And in 969, the Shiite general Jawhar entered Egypt and set up a new capital, Fatimid Cairo (after Fatima, the daughter of the Prophet, from whom the dynasty is descended). Everywhere, new streets, new palaces, new mosques sprang up, crowned by the great Al-Azhar, which was the cornerstone of the faith.

## Al-Azhar

It is only a short distance (a five-minute drive) from the Mosque of Ibn Tulun to Al-Azhar, but a world of difference lies between them! You go in through a doorway with a double arch, passing into an inner courtyard surrounded by elegant arcades, ornamental friezework, a veritable museum of decoration. Here a multitude of different styles and motifs vie for your attention. Look at the beautiful slim columns on which rest great thundering arches! Look up at the forest of minarets, of unequal heights and shapes (even one *double* minaret), and all absolutely covered with delicate, intricate carving, like lacework in stone. Al-Azhar is what Egypt made of Islam.

Of course, it was not done overnight. What you see here is a jumble of styles from many periods, but it was possible only because Cairo became the *permanent* capital of the Shiite faith, and succeeding generations lavished their tribute to their belief. Five times every day the muezzin mounted the tall minaret and issued the call to prayer—but he added a new phrase to the call, a phrase which Ibn Tulun never heard. *"Allah-hu-Akbar* . . . there is no god but God, and Muhammad is his prophet *and Ali is his vice-regent on earth!"*

The story of Ali is typical of all that is chivalrous, valiant, and tragic in the Moslem world. For over a thousand years, people have written poems, told stories, founded youth movements, engraved swords, built shrines, and gone on pilgrimages—all in memory of Ali. Yet who was Ali? A small, chunky, bald-headed man with a swarthy complexion and a long white beard, his sole claim to fame seems to be his kinship to the Prophet—he was cousin and husband of Muhammad's daughter, Fatima.

Ali's place in history is secured by martyrdom. There is nothing the Arabs love so much as a martyr, and Ali filled the role perfectly. After the death of Muhammad, the succession fell on the Prophet's closest friends and followers, among them Abu Bakr, his father-in-law, Umar, Uthman, and Ali. Each in turn was elected to the caliphate after the Prophet's death. By this time, the new Moslem state was big business, and the traditional aristocratic families wanted a share of it—particularly the wealthy Umayyads. The last to profess Islam, they brought a complaint against the election of Ali. The simple, generous man (all Arab

*Partial view of Al-Azhar University in Cairo.*

heroes are simple, generous men) agreed to an arbitration, was tricked, and later murdered with a poisoned saber.

The Umayyads won and established a hereditary caliphate at Damascus. But the followers of Ali demanded that the succession should remain in the family of the Prophet, that is, the descendants of Ali and his wife Fatima. It was this cause which the wily al-Shi promoted two hundred years later when he put forward the claim of Said ibn Husayn to be a descendant of Ali. It is impossible today to establish authenticity of the claim. But at the time it was passionately believed by half the Moslem world.

As a result, the Azhar became not only the shrine but also the school of the Shiite faith. Even today, it is customary to see a teacher seated on a sheepskin in one of the arcades, with his back against a pillar, and his babouches (soft shoes worn in the mosque only) before him. He prefers to sit barefoot. Around him are gathered three rows of auditors, young men and boys, also barefoot and with their babouches before them like a string of ripe bananas. This is an Islamic school.

In early times, this was all the instruction that was available, and it is remarkable that people received their whole education from the Koran. This book, nearly as long as the New Testament, which is believed to be dictated to Muhammad by God, had to be memorized in its entirety. Then it was analyzed and copied out by hand. In the process, an entire generation learned to read and write. And to this day we can see such schools, all seated in a circle on the ground, swaying their bodies back and forth from the waist as they recite the Koran.

Now the Azhar has grown into the most important university in the Islamic world. It has over 1220 teachers, and over 20,000 students from thirty countries are studying within its walls. Some of them live outside in various parts of the town, but many reside in the Azhar itself. They are divided according to nationalities and are housed in *riwaks*, simple sleeping-and-study halls. The higher studies are still theology, Islamic law, and Arabic. But nowadays history, mathematics, chemistry, biology, and astronomy are also taught. A full period of study is fifteen years and can be as long as twenty-two years. And the condition of admission is still a knowledge of the Koran by heart!

*A vegetable seller in Cairo. A moment before, he vigorously protested against having his picture taken. But after a small purchase he was all smiles.*

## Old Cairo

How fresh and wonderful it must have been to be here when General Jawhar first laid out the new streets of the Fatimid city! Today these streets have fallen upon evil times, and the poorest sectors of the populace crowd, whole families to a single room, into the former palaces of the caliphs and their favorites. Walk through the Khan el Khalili Bazaar, where history is written on every stone. But you must leave your valuables at home and keep a watchful eye for anyone who may accost you. On all sides you will see poverty and misery at its worst. The massive, gray, medieval walls line the narrow streets like the banks of a rushing river: fierce, arrogant men in tattered galabiyas; black-gowned women, their faces hidden behind a veil; ragged, screaming barefoot children—all pour by, taking possession of the entire street in a solid mass through which an occasional car creeps apologetically along. Some of the buildings have been turned into shops, mere crannies in the wall, displaying meat, fruit, vegetables; a shopkeeper sits plucking a live chicken, which escapes squawking under the feet of passersby; another man beats a sad-eyed donkey that has fallen to its knees under an incredible load of furniture; and soon a horde of beggar children, all in seeming fun, but with a menacing note in their voices, gather around pointing and shrieking at the "foreigner." In a moment of panic you may push one out of your way. The child falls. And a terrible silence descends on the street. If you are lucky, a policeman may get you safely away. But you will dream for a long time of Fatimid Cairo!

And yet there is so much to see. Some of the finest medieval gates in the world were built to guard the Fatimid city. On the north, Bab-al-Nasar and Bab-al-Futuh still stand, bereft of walls on either side—two lonely citadels keeping watch over ancient memories. They resemble Roman gates, being immensely deep, and containing in their interiors enormous vaults for stores, ammunitions, and armed men. Between the watchtowers are wide embrasures through which archers could keep watch—or shoot—and the passages on the battlements over the portcullis contain apertures for pouring boiling oil on the besiegers. The view from the battlements is splendid and is perhaps the only place in Old Cairo where you are able to use your camera unrestricted. The popular prejudice against the camera is almost a frenzy in Cairo, and in these days

*Minaret of the Mosque of al-Hakim in Cairo dates from the eleventh century.*

of spy mania, a camera works almost like a lightning conductor on the passions of the mob.

## Al-Hakim

From Bab-al-Nasar, you look directly down into the ruins of the Mosque of Al-Hakim. The general decay that hangs about all the mosques of Cairo is a surprise to anyone from the West, who may interpret this as an indication of the decay of Islam. It may be well to recall, therefore, the comments of a Spanish traveler of the eleventh century, Ibn Said, which might pass for the description of a contemporary:

> I entered a mosque of beautiful dimensions and ancient construction. which had no paneling; poorly cared-for mats hung from the walls and lay on the floor. Here merchants sold all sorts of sweets, cakes and other dainties that the customers ate on the spot without any shame, for this had become their habit. A great number of little boys carried jars of water which they passed around among the people who were eating and who threw their refuse on the ground in corners and on the walls. Children played in the court. The walls were marked with the vulgar lines of various graffiti, done in coal and brick and traced by people of the lowest class. Yet, in spite of everything, in this building one breathed an air of joy, of happiness with life, of peace of soul that was not encountered in the great mosque in Seville, with its rich paneling and its garden in the central court. I thought about this strange charm that came through, the reasons for which were not immediately understood. . . .

However, there is a special reason for the utter dereliction of the Mosque of Al-Hakim. It is generally believed in the Moslem world that its builder was accursed for daring to proclaim himself God. The sixth Fatimid caliph, Al-Hakim, embarked on a policy of persecution. He killed several of his grand viziers, or prime ministers, and forced unbelievers— Christians and Jews—to wear black robes and ride on donkeys. He ordered the destruction of the Church of the Holy Sepulcher in Jerusalem—the first of several events that would eventually set off the holocaust of the Crusades. One year before his death, Al-Hakim declared himself the

*View of a village near Cairo.*

incarnation of God (which a sect of Islam, the Druses, still believe him to be). He was assassinated while out riding one day in A.D. 1021.

## The Fatimid City

But the coming and going of the caliphs made little difference to the life of the people in Fatimid times. Throughout medieval, and even modern, history, the backbone of the populace was made up of ancient Egyptian stock, that is, Arabized Copts. In Islamic times, the administration of the country was in Christian hands. Indeed, it is an unaccountable fact that al-Hakim's order to destroy the Holy Sepulcher was signed by his Christian secretary, ibn-Abdun.

It is not surprising, then, that these houses in Khan el Khalili are the medieval successors of the ancient houses of the Pharaohs pictured on the tombs. Many have four or five stories; the lower ones made of stone and the upper stories of light wood, palm fronds, reeds, and earth. They have terraces where the inhabitants can cool off in the evening.

If you step through one of the narrow doorways that open on the street, you will find yourself in a large courtyard, which once was the real center of the house. Outside, all is bare and forbidding, as if to discourage prying eyes. As a further discouragement, the street doorway may have a jog in it, cutting off the direct view from the street.

Once in the courtyard, however, you can see how these princes and wealthy merchants lived. Around you are ranged rows of balconies, with many stairways and doors of parti-colored marble. Moucharabies—projecting windows or balconies enclosed with grilles of carved beads—once concealed bevies of laughing women. Such big houses were necessary for the many women of the harem and their innumerable children.

In Fatimid times, there would be a fountain splashing in the center of the court, surrounded by exotic trees in tubs, with songbirds in their branches. Here the women and children spent most of their time, secure from the outside world. The houses did not contain a great variety of furniture. Just as in Ancient Egypt, people sat on benches covered with cushions. Beds did not exist, only mats. But there would be many chests filled with cloth of gold, rugs, and valuables. The wealth of these householders was in their rich cloth.

Everything is changed today. The courtyard you stand in is now a slum; the apartments of the harem have become squalid tenements, where large families of three and four generations live packed together in a single room. And your intrusion is not likely to be appreciated. Take your camera and your memories of Fatimid Cairo and go—fast!

But if the houses of the courtiers were splendid, how much more magnificent was the palace of the caliph himself! In the year 1167, the ambassadors of the Kingdom of Jerusalem made an unprecedented visit to the caliph. The record of this visit still exists and paints an almost incredible picture of Fatimid luxury. The envoys were met by the grand vizier and shown through courtyards paved with marble and set off with gold trimmings. The rafters of the porticoes were all covered with gold. And at every turn they were met by guards dressed in shining gold armor.

Then they came to a vast room divided in two by a hanging curtain covered with figures of birds and other animals, and people, all set with rubies, emeralds, and other precious stones. The room appeared to be empty. But the grand vizier prostrated himself three times and suddenly, "as if by a bolt of lightning," cords raised the curtain and the child caliph was seen sitting on his throne.

This gorgeous scene, which overwhelmed the crude and barbarous Crusaders, was, however, the very last flicker of Fatimid glory. The boy caliph, al-Adid, was soon to die, like so many others of his line before him, strangled by silken cords or buried alive in the walls of the palace, a victim of the intrigues of the all-powerful viziers. For the time had come to make way for a new and more vigorous hero on the stage of history.

## Saladin

His name was Saladin, and no one in Cairo was ever to forget it, for the Citadel he built overshadows the daily lives of the Egyptian people to this day. Built on a spur of the Mokattam Hills to the south of the city—just a ten-minute walk from the bazaar—the tremendous bulk of this medieval fortress looms high on the skyline. For the moment you should ignore the great dome of the Muhammad Ali Mosque and the pencil-like minarets that have made this site one of the most picturesque in the world.

Saladin did not build those minarets, and he would have scorned the elegant architecture of later and more luxurious generations. For the Commander of the Faithful was a stern warrior, dedicated to the triumph of Islam, and he had no use for artists, infidels, or heretics. Born in an armed camp, in the domains of the Caliph of Baghdad, he grew up in a world of war. There were the intrigues of the atabegs and emirs who were vassals of the caliph. And then there was the unremitting struggle against the onset of the Christian Crusades for possession of the Holy Land. And lastly, there was the hatred of all orthodox believers for the heretical Fatimids of Cairo.

In this situation, it is perhaps not surprising to find the Fatimids receiving ambassadors from the Crusaders with a view toward an alliance against the indomitable Saladin. But the alliance was short-lived. With typical perfidy, the Crusaders abandoned their allies in Cairo to the mercy of Saladin when his hordes descended on the city. And in

*The Citadel, Cairo. The walls and gate were built by Saladin. The Mosque of Muhammad Ali stands above it.*

the inevitable massacre that followed the siege, it was the Christian Copts who suffered the greatest loss of life.

Saladin restored Egypt to orthodoxy. The Christians were proscribed and compelled to pay a tax, the *dhimi* tax, just for being alive. The Fatimid heresy was rigorously extirpated. No longer did the muezzin call the faithful to prayer in the name of "Ali, vice-regent of God on earth." And the city and country were garrisoned by fierce Turkish warriors who scorned the ancient, sybaritic civilization.

Up and down the Mokattam Hills, a forlorn gang of Christian prisoners, many of them Franks (as the Moslems called all Westerners), was soon toiling, dragging stones for the new Citadel. It was a labor such as Egypt had seen many times before, and there is a sad irony in the fact that many of these stones came from the smaller pyramid of Gizeh, at least twenty miles away!

As you walk around the forbidding bastions and through the massive entrance gate into Saladin's Citadel, you may note with surprise the Norman features of this grim fortress. Perhaps Saladin used a Christian architect from France. In this way, the interaction began between West and East, as each learned from the other. But you cannot leave the Citadel of Cairo without a sigh of regret for the fate of those men from Normandy, Lorraine, and Auvergne who came to the East to save the True Cross from the infidel and stayed behind to build a fortress for the sultan.

For Saladin was now sultan. With characteristic opportunism, he proceeded to found a new dynasty, the Ayyubid, which soon threw off all real allegiance to the caliph in Baghdad. From this time on, Egypt was to become a military state, garrisoned by soldiers and run like an army, with headquarters in the Citadel.

### The Mamelukes

As with most military dictatorships, there was constant struggle for the succession. The Ayyubid Dynasty lasted barely eighty years before it was overthrown by its own slaves, the Mamelukes. The story is a strange one and worth retelling. The Mamelukes were, in the main, Circassians, uprooted from their native land in the Caucasus and forced to serve, on account of their height, bearing, and perhaps their fair complexion, as bodyguards to the sultan. And since these sultans were permitted to have many wives under the Moslem law, Mameluke women frequently entered the harem.

One such Mameluke woman, by the name of Shajar al-Durr, changed the course of history when she seized the throne for herself on the death of her husband, Sultan al-Salih (1249 A.D.). For the third time, following Hatshepsut and Cleopatra, a woman sat on the throne of Egypt. For eighty days the sultana ruled. She had coins struck in her name, and had her name mentioned as caliph in the Friday prayers at the mosque. Then, in order to crush her opponents, she married her commander in chief, Izz-al-Din-Aybak.

But the sultana had no intention to take a back seat. She kept her husband in subjection during the seven years of his reign, and when he showed signs of taking another wife, she had him murdered in his bath after a ball game. Immediately afterward, she herself was battered to death with the wooden shoes of the slave women of Aybak's first wife, and her body was cast down from the tower. This is one of the darker tales the gray stones of the Citadel have to tell.

The Mamelukes ruled Egypt for 267 years, until the Turkish invasion in 1517. It is hard to imagine today what life must have been like in those terrible days. The whole of Egypt became the personal property of the sultans, and the people were treated as their slaves; in other words, they were the slaves of their own former slaves.

The personal history of one of the most famous of these Mamelukes—Baybars, who ruled from 1260 to 1277—will show just what it took to become a sultan. Baybars was general of the army during the onslaught of the Mongol conqueror Hulagu Khan, whose hordes descended on the Middle East like locusts out of central Asia. Baybars' victory at the battle of Ayn Jalut may have saved the West from being overrun at that time, and deflected the course of history.

As a reward, Baybars expected to be given a fief by the sultan, but he was disappointed. In revenge, the general launched a conspiracy against his liege lord. While a fellow conspirator kissed the sultan's hand, Baybars ran him through the neck with a sword. The murdered sultan was succeeded by his murderer. And so it went from generation to generation. A large number of sultans met their deaths in this fashion. The average reign of the Mamelukes was less than six years each.

A nightmare time! And yet, and yet—what is this noble gateway on el Zahir Street, not far from Cairo's modern railway station? It is the Sultan Baybars Mosque, your guide will tell you. Look at the splendid simplicity of this portal, with its beautifully proportioned arch decorated with a double-zigzag motif. Then pass through into the gardens of the mosque. Around you is calm, peace, the glory of flowers and trees, of rich stone and marble laid out in the traditional plan of the arcaded sanctuary. It was Baybars himself who designed this mosque, sending camels, buffalo, and oxen to quarries in every corner of Egypt to bring the stone and marble. The ex-slave and murderer was also a dreamer and a builder.

Most of the sultans were treacherous and bloodthirsty; several could not read or write. Barquq (1382–1398) was the only one with a Moslem father. Barsbay (1422–1438), a slave of Barquq, could not even speak Arabic. When his doctors could not cure his fatal illness, he had two of them beheaded. Inlal (1453–1460), another slave of Barquq, could not recite the first *surah* (chapter) of the Koran without a mistake and had to trace his signature over the writing of a secretary. Yalbay (1467) was not only illiterate but also insane.

Everywhere in Cairo, the ghosts of the Mamelukes are waiting to haunt you. They still dominate the modern metropolis with their splendid monuments, which make the squat, huddled buildings of later times look shabby in comparison. The Mosque of Sultan Qalaun, the Monastery of Baybars II, the Mausoleum of Emirs Sanjar and Salat, the Blue Mosque, the College of Sultan Hassan . . . Stop a moment at this last one.

You are in a narrow street at the edge of Citadel Square. The gray walls rise steeply over your head like a towering cliff of stone intersected with narrow grooves for windows. The facade of the doorway is topped with an enormous honeycomb that looks as though it would come crashing down on your head, and serves to increase the effect of height. Mount the double stairway to the entrance and pass within. You are entering Moslem Egypt's most perfect monument, the one most worthy to stand beside the outstanding landmarks of the civilization of the Pharaohs.

"To appreciate this monument," says the art critic Gaston Weit, "one must acquire a long familiarity through assiduous contemplation; it is by looking at it for a long time under its every aspect that one discovers its breathtaking beauty and royal majesty."

Stay then, if you are lucky enough to walk on these stones, and try to resolve the riddle of how, out of the blood and cruelty of an insane civilization, a portion of the world's great heritage of beauty was born. Of Sultan Hassan (1347–1361), nothing else is remembered. He was a puppet in the hands of his own slaves, who eventually replaced him.

But to all things there comes an end. If you are to witness this end, you must make your way to the Bab Zuweila Gate, at the edge of the Khan el Khalili Bazaar. Grim, proud, the twin bastions of this gate, topped by the minarets of a mosque, still look down on a motley throng of merchants and travelers, and sad-eyed donkeys with impossible loads that wend their way through the narrow gateway.

On April 14, in the year 1517, the last of the Mameluke sultans, Tuman Bey, was brought to this place in chains. His captors were the Ottoman Turks, whose armies, under Selim I, were sweeping through the Middle East from Persia to the Valley of the Nile. Captured after a spirited defense of the city, Tuman Bey was given a public execution. A noose was tied around his neck and drawn up over one of the parapets of the gate. The rope broke and Tuman fell to the foot of the gate. Drawn up a second time, the same thing happened. Only on the third attempt was the Mameluke finally dispatched.

Later, at one of the popular shadow plays, a kind of puppet show for which Cairo has been famous over the centuries, the conqueror, Sultan Selim, was shown a reenactment of the scene. Three times the doll, representing Tuman Bey, was strung up over the toy gate. The Ottoman Sultan found it very amusing when the rope broke twice. He rewarded the producer with a sum of money (the equivalent of about $900), and said, "When we leave for Stamboul, come with us so my son can see this show!"

# Ottoman Twilight

## Conquerors and Foreigners

Wherever you go in Egypt and look at the gigantic monuments of the past, with their often macabre stories, one question must frequently recur to your mind: Where were the *Egyptians* when all this happened? For it is a truly extraordinary thing to consider that, in all the history of Egypt during the past three thousand years, the Egyptians themselves had almost no part. From the time of Thutmose III (about 1500 B.C.), it became the habit of Egyptian rulers to import foreigners to run the country. Eventually the rulers—like the Ptolemies—were not even Egyptian themselves. Cleopatra was a Greek. The Romans and the Byzantines ran Egypt as a colony. Even the Arab conquerors did not mingle with the local population when they settled in Egypt. The Mamelukes became a vast foreign-born governing class, who did their own fighting and did not even impress the Egyptians into their army.

And all the time the millions of fellahin toiled at the shaduf, irrigating the fields, washing clothes at the canal edge, or standing up to the waist in slime, cleaning the silt out of the drainage canals. It was their labor that provided food and plenty for the conquerors. It was their taxes that built the great shining palaces shimmering in marble and luxurious in rugs. It was their acquiescence that later built the banks, the railways, the Suez Canal—all for the benefit of foreign businessmen. Why did they do it?

*Sugarcane grows in Upper Egypt, near Aswan.*

As you get to know the Egyptian people, you find there is an essential tranquillity about them. This may come as a surprise to those who are accustomed to see them in crowds shaking angry fists and demanding the heads of traitors or enemies. But this is an effect of demagoguery which is a manifestation of modern times.

From time immemorial, the Egyptian people have been content to inhabit their great valley as they did in ancient times—surrounded by the golden walls of wheat, the brown mud villages, the green of the big palms; never looking beyond the horizon of their world, nor asking more than their good earth yielded. Not for them the conquering mania of the Aryan or Semitic races. They never sought to dominate others (even Thutmose used Asiatic levies for his wars in Syria, and Nubians for

*The people of New Nubia look very much as Old Nubians have looked for thousands of years.*

his conquests above the Third Cataract of the Nile). And it is a matter of record that the Egyptians never mounted a popular revolution in their history until the end of the nineteenth century. The horrors we hear of, therefore, in Egypt's long story, are foreign horrors, enacted against the eternally peaceful scene of Egypt.

The advent of Ottoman Turkey in A.D 1517 made little difference to this pattern. As a matter of fact, apart from the appointment of a Turkish pasha or governor, and the annual tribute that was sent to Constantinople, life went on as before. Even the Mameluke emirs, who were now a very numerous class. were retained throughout the provinces "in the interests of efficiency." No one had ever thought of letting the fellahin run their own country.

The years rolled by while Egypt slept. These were years, during the sixteenth, seventeenth, and eighteenth centuries, when the Western world was on the move. The printing press was invented in Mainz, the Rights of Man were proclaimed in Paris, the spinning jenny was in use in Lancashire—but of all these things Egypt lay in darkest ignorance.

## Napoleon in Egypt

The awakening came with a salvo from the guns of Napoleon's flagship *l'Orient* off Alexandria on July 15, 1798. The Mameluke cavalrymen made a brave show, brandishing their naked sabers in the air as they charged the French massed infantry, but the slaughter was inevitable. Napoleon, who had evidently decided to begin building his empire in Egypt, was looking for a popular rising against the Mamelukes, in answer to his call of *liberté, égalité, fraternité.* He was disappointed.

The printing press on which his proclamation was issued caused intense interest—it was the first printing press ever seen in Egypt—but the message went unheeded. Napoleon was received with the indifference the Egyptians have always exhibited toward conquerors, before and since. On the steps of the palace of Elfy Bey, in Cairo's Esvekiah Gardens, he appeared in Egyptian costume under a gigantic turban, and harangued the populace on the Rights of Man. All to no purpose. Egypt turned its back on its "liberator."

The scene, as Napoleon saw it, was described by one of his commanders, Vivant Denon, as follows:

> . . . the domes and minarets of three hundred mosques rose from the smoke of cooking fires. The Citadel lifted its gray battlements proudly over the warren of houses and streets. And in the desert beyond appeared the three pyramids of Gizeh. But, seen up close, these noble prospects disintegrated. Rubbish lay about on every side. The haunt of scavenging dogs and cats . . . and in the worst slums it was hard to say which were the ruins of fallen buildings and which the hovels of the present generation. Not a single fine street [laments Denon] not a single beautiful building . . . they build as little as they can help. They never repair anything.

Napoleon set about changing all this. He brought with him from France an army of savants and engineers. New streets were to be laid out, a canal was to be cut at Suez between the Mediterranean and the Red Sea, the Rosetta Stone was to be deciphered to unlock the secrets of the hieroglyphics. All these things were done—but not by Napoleon. The British under Nelson caught up with the French fleet at Aboukir Bay and destroyed it. Napoleon beat a quick retreat to France.

## Muhammad Ali

The man who benefited most from this history-making development was the son of an Albanian farmer in the ranks of the Turkish Army sent to Egypt to defeat Napoleon. His name was Muhammad Ali. A small man with a dark complexion and a reddish beard, he could neither read nor write. But in the chaos of Egypt at that time he quickly rose to power. By playing off the Mamelukes against the Turks, he drew the Egyptian people to his side, and they soon ejected the Turkish governor altogether and demanded that Muhammad Ali rule them. The Turks could only weakly consent and make him governor.

And so Egypt had yet another foreigner to rule it. But it was different this time. For the first time in over two thousand years, *Egyptians* made the choice. No Egyptian had the education—and the daring—to make Egypt independent. But they chose Muhammad Ali to do it. For

*Cairo University at Gizeh.*

the first time, Egyptians were enrolled in the armed forces and even became officers. Great events were to follow.

Of course, Muhammad Ali was a tyrant, just as any Eastern potentate was expected to be. In the museum of the Citadel today you may see a model of him, sitting cross-legged on his divan, smoking his inevitable hookah, or water pipe. He is conducting a court of justice. At his judgment, the accused may be taken away and flogged or sent to the galleys. At a single sign—a horizontal motion of the hand—with no words spoken, the unlucky man may have his throat cut then and there. Muhammad Ali was a man of swift action.

A perfect example of his method—and this happened in the first half of the nineteenth century—was his handling of the problem of the Mamelukes. They had grown so numerous that they were a constant hazard to his administration. So one day, Muhammad Ali invited five hundred of the leading Mamelukes to dine with him in the Citadel. Afterward, they departed in a body. In the narrow road from the Citadel, which passed the Sultan Hassan Mosque, they were trapped and murdered by Muhammad Ali's men, who were firing down on them from above. The massacre of their fellows throughout the country brought the death toll to several thousands.

Yet this man was looked upon with affection (and still is) by every Egyptian. Look back at the Citadel and you will see why. There stands the most splendid monument in modern Cairo—the Muhammad Ali Mosque. Soaring above the Citadel so as to dwarf the walls of Saladin, there stands this miracle of Baroque architecture: the powerful dome, the unbelievable soaring spires, which have become an essential part of the skyline of Cairo and as much "Egypt" as the pyramids. Inside the mosque, after walking over acres of deep-pile carpet and admiring the ostentation of marble and alabaster, stop a moment beside a small tomb surrounded by a gilded balustrade and covered in rich tapestries. Here lies Muhammad Ali.

What Muhammad Ali gave to Egypt and for what he is mainly remembered is dignity. For the first time since the conquest of Alexander the Great in 332 B.C., Egypt was a nation. The foul-smelling streets of Cairo gave way to new, impressive avenues of stone buildings—the modern Cairo we see today. The canals, some disused for two thousand years, were redug and twenty thousand waterwheels installed. The tax farmers, who had *bought* the right to squeeze the fellahin, were called off. And the foundation of the future was laid by the introduction of long-staple cotton, which transformed the economy of Egypt. Muhammad Ali founded a dynasty that was to lead into the future. But, unfortunately, Muhammad Ali's successors left much to be desired, especially Ismael, who acceded to the throne as khedive in 1863.

## Ismael

Although westernized, with a Parisian education, Ismael's outward appearance must have been rather alarming. Even the official portraits on the wall had difficulty in disguising the short, ungainly body and the grotesque head covered with a tarboosh (a red hat similar to a fez) large enough to conceal two floppy, misshapen ears. His face was half covered with tufts of red beard, one of his eyes wandered uncontrollably in its socket.

The palace of Ismael tells of his love for splendor. As you wander from hall to hall—there are five hundred of them, all glittering from top to bottom with tessellated marble and hung with velvet draperies, magnificent tapestries, and mirrors, and absolutely reeking with the kind of opulence that today is considered the very acme of bad taste—your reactions are apt to be violent. How was all this wealth squeezed out of the poor people of Egypt? the visitor asks, remembering the thousands of mud-floored villages along the Nile.

Ismael's answer, if he were here to speak for himself, would be that European bankers had *lent* him the money in exchange for certain investments in Egypt. This is quite true. What's more, these investments were designed to better the economy of Egypt greatly. A railway was constructed from Alexandria to Port Suez, thereby shortening the route to India, which formerly went by sea around the Cape of Good Hope.

Even more ambitiously, a canal was dug from Port Said on the Mediterranean to Suez on the Red Sea, which would take ships traveling in both directions. This enterprise caught the imagination of the entire world. Verdi composed an opera, *Aïda*, for the occasion, and Ismael now built an opera house to stage it. The Empress Eugénie of France was the first to sail through the canal in 1869, followed by Ismael girt with a scimitar blazing with jewels, the Emperor of Austria, and other members of European royalty. The Prince and Princess of Wales (later to become King Edward VII and Queen Alexandra) were present at the opening of the sluices joining the two seas and separating Africa from Asia.

## The First Suez Crisis

All this was very grand indeed. What Ismael would try not to tell you, however, is that he proved to be a very bad businessman. By the time he had purchased the shares in the Suez Canal Company to which he was obligated under the terms of the agreement, he had almost paid for the

*The palace of Tewfik, a nineteenth-century ruler of Egypt. Note moucharabies (dark portion over the entrance).*

canal himself! And yet the rights to the property, the operation and dues of the canal were to remain in the hands of a foreign company based in Paris—for ninety-nine years! This was the basis for a quarrel that was to poison Egypt's relations with the West for a century to come.

To Ismael, of course, none of this mattered very much. The money he spent in these transactions came from the Egyptian Treasury, which was replenished with loans from Paris and London at interest rates up to 30 percent. And when the creditors closed in, in 1879, he cleaned out the cash in the Treasury and, taking his valuables and a sum of about $15 million, boarded his yacht at Alexandria and sailed away into the sunset, never to return.

Ismael's son, Tewfik, had to stay and face the music. Young and inexperienced as he was, he turned for help to the source of all his country's troubles—the Europeans. Britain and France, the two countries most deeply involved in Egypt, were only too happy to establish dual control, with full authority over the country's budget, in order to recover their money (with interest).

All this caused much debate in the coffeehouses frequented by the intellectuals, at Al-Azhar University, where the influence of the foreign-hating *ulema,* the Moslem teachers, was paramount, and, above all, in the barrack-room messes of the Egyptian Army. Now, at last, the policy of Mohammed Ali of recruiting the fellahin for armed service was going to bear fruit. Most fellahin in uniform were merely in the rank and file, but a few had already risen to commissioned rank. Among them was a colonel named Ahmed Bey Arabi.

The son of a village sheikh, Colonel Arabi spoke for Egypt. Even his enemy, Sir Auckland Colvin, described him as calm, serious, resolute, but not a practical man. Arabi recognized that the Egyptian regiments under his command possessed the power to overthrow the foreign stranglehold on the country. It was on a day in May, 1882, when the sheikh's son presented himself at the palace in Cairo with a petition demanding a constitution and social reform. When his request was rejected, Arabi threatened to blow up the Suez Canal and cancel Egypt's foreign debts. He was promptly arrested, and the Army revolted.

In a dramatic confrontation at the Abdin Palace, the khedive surrendered abjectly and appointed a new government, with Colonel Arabi as Minister of War. But this was only to gain time. As soon as British and French warships appeared off Alexandria, the European powers demanded the dismissal of the nationalist government and the deportation of Arabi.

All those who think history does not repeat itself should read the events of the summer of 1882. There you will find the explanation of all that took place exactly seventy-four years later. The circumstances, the events, the personalities in each confrontation between the European nationalists in the West were very much the same. The major difference was that in 1956 world opinion was with Egypt; in 1882 it was not.

In mid-August, Sir Garnet Wolseley landed in Egypt and occupied the Suez Canal before Arabi was able to blow it up. The British Army caught the Egyptian Army literally napping at Tell-el-Kebir and after a short battle of an hour or two, ten thousand Egyptians were left dead on the field. Colonel Arabi surrendered and was exiled to Ceylon.

## Western Business Interests Take Over

*"Plus ça change, plus c'est la même chose,"* the French are fond of saying. Not so much changes in the world as some wishful thinkers would like to believe—least of all, human nature. The Egyptians in 1882 had been miserably tricked, imposed upon, and fleeced by the foreigners. The wonder is not that the worm turned but that it did not do so long before. Why was Arabi too late at the Canal (he had two months to fulfill his threat to destroy it)? Why was the Egyptian Army surprised asleep in their tents (as they were by the Israeli planes in June, 1967)?

The answer would require a long analysis of the Egyptian character and the factors that determine the rise and fall of civilizations. The most famous historian of our time, Arnold Toynbee, sees the root of decline in most civilizations as self-caused. The Arabic society, he says, "may have been destroyed by the incubus of a parasitic nomad institution in a non-nomad world—the slave ascendancy of the Egyptian Mamelukes—unless this society affords a solitary case of destruction by an alien assailant."

Put into everyday terms, this means that the Egyptian people had lost confidence in themselves. The incredibly long foreign occupation had sapped the essential dignity of the man by the shaduf, so that he no longer remembered that once he had been a builder of pyramids. True, the last of the Mamelukes were gone. But their place had been taken by the latest of empire builders, the Western businessmen. By 1882, Egypt was crawling with them. In the major cities, the foreign population was one in twelve, or ninety thousand over the country as a whole—and not one of these ninety thousand was subject to Egyptian taxation. All the major national resources—the cotton crop, the overland railway traffic to Port Suez, the Suez Canal—were fiefs of European industrial empires. The government itself was in receivership to the boards of European banking houses.

The instinctive reaction to this situation was self-destructive. Because they were fleeced, Egyptians in turn fleeced the foreigner. Foreigners learned to watch their wallets in public places and to demand the strongest punishment for thievery. In the courts, which were run by Europeans, the European was always right; the Egyptian was always wrong. European contempt for the Egyptian population was undisguised.

The feeling was mutual. Everywhere the foreigners were hated with an unholy zeal. In Alexandria, during the torrid summer of 1882, agitators ran wild in the streets, shouting, "O Moslems, kill the Christians!" Several hundred people were killed or wounded, some fifty Europeans among them. The British press was not long in placing the blame on Colonel Arabi—who had no knowledge of the riots—and characterized him as a madman akin to a crazed monkey.

So began the long misunderstanding between Egypt and the West, according to which the Egyptians saw Europeans as a new storm of locusts that was eating up the country for their own profit, and the Europeans saw the Egyptians as a subhuman species incapable of conducting their own affairs and dangerously anarchical if allowed off the leash. It was a tragic case of the clash of two cultures out of tune and out of time with each other.

*An aerial view of Port Said and a section of the Suez Canal.*

# The Struggle with Britain

## Life in Heliopolis

The British residents of Cairo (who until lately constituted a large and agreeable society) liked to live in big villas at Heliopolis, the Garden City, where the breeze is cool. Their gates always had a guard, in uniform and fez, who let you in if you tinkled the bell and showed a calling card. The villas were set in spacious gardens surrounded by high walls with broken glass along the top to keep "undesirable elements" out. Purple bougainvilleas hung down in profuse masses over the garden walls and from the balconies and balustrades. Palm trees provided pleasant shade for tea parties ("tiffin" was served at five o'clock) on lawns, which were kept watered by a legion of gardeners throughout the hot season.

Over tea—or it might be a gin and tonic—these British residents talked with fond affection for Egypt. They had a host of Egyptian friends who, like themselves, went calling in their carriages each day at the appropriate hour. This pasha and that bey and dear Madame So-and-So all agreed with the British that things simply could not be better. The value of land was increasing daily, and everyone was in a hurry to build more villas. In season, the succession of balls and fêtes was simply unending. All the best people were sending their sons to public school in Britain and their daughters to finishing school in Switzerland, and society was becoming terribly up to date.

*Cairo is a modern city as well as an ancient monument.*

*Modern bridge over the Nile at Cairo.*

The following conversation was overheard by a French traveler at the Turf Club, the most fashionable resort in Cairo for the British community, at the turn of the century:

> "My dear fellow, business is A.1. Egypt has entered on a period of prosperity scarcely credible. We are making money hand over fist, everyone is in the swim. You will see for yourself—from one end of Egypt to the other you will hear the same story. The Government has been able to reduce taxation and increase the salaries of its employees, big and little. The golden age has arrived."
>
> —from *New Egypt* by A. B. de Guerville

And it was all quite true. From the depths of dereliction and decay, Britain at the turn of the twentieth century had brought Egypt to the very height of prosperity. The arable land was vastly increased with the building of many irrigation dams across the Nile; railway lines were constantly being extended, and work on the port at Alexandria simply could not keep up with the fleets of shipping in the crowded harbor.

If all this was done a little irregularly, what of it? The fact was that the British occupation of Egypt had no basis in law other than conquest. By operating behind the scenes, so that all orders were issued by the khedive and his government, the British did not need to show their hand. The only British official in Egypt who had any power was Lord Cromer, the consul general. Did it seem a bit farfetched that a king and government should take its orders from a foreign consul general? "But of what can we complain of Britain?" asked one Egyptian prime minister. "To her we owe our wealth and prosperity. She has treated us with consideration and justice to which none of the great powers accustomed us."

## The Massacre of Denshawy

Yet something seemed wrong. A frigid chill settled over the tiffin parties when one day in June of 1906, the news came of a massacre at Denshawy. In this obscure village in the Delta, a party of British army officers had been amusing themselves shooting pigeons when they were disarmed by a hostile crowd of villagers who objected to having their pigeons shot. One rifle was discharged in the struggle and a woman and several local men were wounded. The officers made their escape, but on returning with reinforcements they found one of their own number dead from head wounds and sunstroke. They immediately seized a villager who was standing nearby and clubbed him to death. Fifty-two others were seized and turned over to the Egyptian courts, which acquiesced to a demand for heavy sentences. (Four villagers were executed, the rest given sentences of hard labor.)

How could this happen? Obviously, most British residents never could understand it. They came to regard the mass of the Egyptian people (that is, other than this pasha and that bey and dear Madame So-and-So) as fickle and ungrateful and undeserving of all that had been done for them. They probably never reflected for a moment, as they read the *Egyptian Gazette*, that Egyptians were less than content with a budget that ensured quick fortunes for a ruling class of effendi, or landowners, mostly Turks, Armenians, Circassians, French, and English, while less than 1½ percent of the total budget was spent on education and health. What it comes to is just this: what the British thought good enough for Egypt did not seem good enough to the 70 percent of the population who produced the wealth and paid the taxes.

After Denshawy, the misunderstanding between British and Egyptians deepened. The First World War created an impassable gulf. When Turkey sided with the Central Powers (Germany, Austria-Hungary, and Bulgaria), the fiction of Egyptian allegiance to Constantinople could no longer be maintained, and Britain declared Egypt an outright British Protectorate. Egypt contributed a large quantity of men and money to the war effort. Why was it, then, Egyptian nationalists asked, that the bedouin Arabs, who had fought a brief campaign against Turkey with Lawrence, should be given their independence, while the Egyptians, the descendants of one of the oldest civilizations in the world, should remain in subjection?

## The Ikhwan

As the Paris Peace Conference met in 1919, university students at Al-Azhar streamed into the streets; trains, telegraphs, and railways were sabotaged; British troops had to be called out, and several rioters were shot. The result was an agreement in 1922 whereby Britain recognized Egyptian sovereignty over domestic affairs, while Egypt was pledged to respect British rights in the Canal, the courts, and elsewhere. The khedive became king, a parliament was established—and everything went on as before.

The compromise pleased no one, particularly not the Egyptian nationalists, who now took shelter in the new Wafd party. They refused to accept the solution that still left the foreigner in control of the country's economy. At the election of the first parliament in 1924, the Wafd won a stunning victory that reflected the new feeling of unity in the country. This feeling was also reflected that year in the murder of the British commander in chief in Egypt, Sir Lee Stack. At the subsequent trial, the Wafd was exonerated, but the real depth of terrorist sentiment in Egypt was revealed.

The string of murders down the years since Denshawy was no accident. Prime ministers, local pashas, British officials, one after another was found shot in the head, face down in a canal, or in bed with a knife between the shoulder blades. Who or what was behind it all? British public opinion persisted in putting the blame on the lowest dregs of Egyptian society. In fact, it was the work of a highly puritanical secret society known as the Moslem Brotherhood.

The Ikhwan (the brethren), as this society was called by the Arabs throughout the Middle East, caused a shiver of righteous horror in European hearts everywhere. The Ikhwan was everything that a well-brought-up British public school boy despised: a hoard of fanatic, heathen rabble, spreading their prayer mats on the curb at noonday rush hour and holding up traffic while they prostrated themselves toward Mecca. Goodness knows what filthy hovels they came out of, wearing their dirty galabiyas, like striped nightgowns, reeking of onions, spitting, blowing their noses in their fingers, and presuming to shout right in

*The double minaret of Al-Azhar in Cairo.*

113

front of the carriage at the British consul general, "Egypt for the Egyptians!"

How could such people govern themselves? thought the British protectors of Egypt. But these same "protectors" were viewed in an equally unflattering light by the "heathen rabble." To begin with, the Europeans were unbelievers. They were outside the pale of God's chosen people spoken of by the Prophet Muhammad. They defiled the Moslem sabbath (by working on Friday). They desecrated the fasts (by eating and drinking during the month of Ramadan). But, worst of all, they, the infidels, oppressed God's people.

No one who did not read the publications of the nationalists of the time (1930–1933), like the *Majallat-al-Azhar,* the "Journal of the Azhar," can have any idea of how deep and fierce ran the hatred of the West. The basis of this emotion was frustration. Islam was God's kingdom on earth. How was it, then, that infidels had their heels on the necks of the Faithful?

> The first Moslems [said the *Majallat-al-Azhar*] conquered the earth by unceasing activity, and kept it under their control by great and constant striving . . . their scholars were the most learned scholars on earth. Their physicians were the most honored physicians on earth. Those engaged in other fields of learning were the leaders to whom problems were referred for solution. And their craftsmen and artificers were the most skilled of their fellows on earth. . . . There is, then, no question but that Islam's enemies are confuted. Praise be to God!

But how was the injustice to be righted? The answer was given by the founder of the Ikhwan, Hassan el-Banna, a village sheikh who had become a schoolteacher. Looking around him, he saw the weakness of his people. Lacking all education, forgetful of the great heritage of Islam, they were easy prey to their foreign oppressors. He gathered a few kindred spirits around him and taught them the virtues of primitive Islam. "I tried to make this a great general movement," he wrote in his memoirs, "based on science, education, and a spirit of militancy, which are the pillars of the Islamic mission."

Soon he was talking of unleashing his "phalanxes" in a new *jihad,* a holy war. His was not an impossible dream. Hassan el-Banna was the Supreme Guide (his own title) for millions of Egyptians. Many of his followers were of the poorest sort, but even the intellectuals among them wrote of the Supreme Guide in terms of extreme adulation, such as that accorded Hitler and Stalin at about the same time.

It seemed entirely possible that at any moment Hassan el-Banna would unleash his phalanxes of terrorists, each of whom had sworn by Allah to be "a guardian of the Brotherhood, a fighter in the cause of Allah, to listen, to obey, and to fight as best I can." Secret cells were set up throughout the country, engaged in reciting the Koran and learning to use guns, revolvers, and hand grenades.

As the Second World War came to an end, with no improvement in the situation of Egypt, which was still in pawn to foreign banking houses abroad and corrupt politicians at home, the Ikhwan struck. Prime ministers were gunned down almost as soon as they took office. Even the king was no longer safe in his own country. Farouk I, the last of the dynasty of Muhammad Ali, started life as a pampered and petted boy king, on whom everyone's hopes were set. His pictures everywhere bore the subscription "Gloriously Reigning." But now it was known that even he was on the blacklist of the Moslem Brotherhood.

## The State of Israel Is Born

Then came the thunderbolt that temporarily diverted and in the end transformed the situation. On May 14, 1948, the British, who had governed Palestine, as it was then called, under a mandate of the League of Nations, departed, and Israel was created. This was regarded as a direct challenge to all Arab states and to Islam itself. All that the Supreme Guide had preached seemed suddenly come to pass. The foreigners— and the Israelis, from the Moslem point of view, were always regarded as foreigners, financed and sponsored as tools of colonialism—once more had their heels on the necks of the Faithful. The *jihad* was deflected to Palestine.

The first Arab-Israel war was fought mainly by the Egyptian Army and the Arab Legion of Transjordan against the newborn Zionist state. In the first advance, the Egyptian Army reached Bethlehem, making contact with the Jordanians. But there was no unified command to the Arab forces and the Israelis soon formed up in the rear, cutting the lines of communication.

The United Nations arranged a truce, but soon the fighting broke out again and the Egyptian Army was driven steadily back until all it held in Palestine was a small salient at Gaza, crammed with several hundred thousand Arab refugees.

How could it happen? Over and over, young Egyptians in the coffeehouses of Cairo and the villages along the Nile debated this question. The Israelis were outnumbered by the Arabs and Egyptians almost eighty to one. Yet they won. The only answer that Egyptians could agree upon was the one Sheikh el-Banna had supplied: The leadership of the country was corrupt and must be overthrown.

## More Trouble over the Suez

Now the bottomless wellspring of hatred for the West in general and for Britain in particular was channeled into another grievance: the Suez Canal. This long-standing target of the nationalists was peculiarly vulnerable. The 1936 treaty had left a small contingent of British troops manning the Canal, where they were so many sitting ducks. The Ikhwan declared guerrilla war upon this easy target.

The strategy was to deny British troops fresh food and water, and to compel the native labor force to withdraw from the canal zone. By this move, nearly seventy thousand Egyptians were thrown out of work, and sabotage and murder occurred daily in the area. Life in Egypt became intolerable for foreigners. By the autumn of 1951, fear and hatred of foreigners had reached its height.

I myself well remember the atmosphere of doom that hung over the gray, wintry streets of Cairo like a heavy cloud in those days. Ordinary, decent Egyptians, in their gray and white galabiyas, stood in long queues outside the British Embassy and hissed as the hated foreigners went in and out. The peculiarly vicious quality of hatred in this hissing was like a haunting refrain. Old men, even beggars bowed over their canes and leaned forward to spit on your shoes as you stood at the curb waiting for the lights to change.

*Life teems in the back streets of Cairo. Under the umbrellas, merchants have their stalls.*

All communication between Cairo and the canal zone, sixty miles away, was cut off. To travel from the capital to British headquarters in Ismailia was like crossing a front line in wartime. I would hire a taxi, and paint "foreign correspondent" in Egyptian characters all over it. The road, which lay across the desert, was thick with army units, the foremost of which were in weapon pits. After a stretch of about two miles of empty desert, I would sight the first British patrol.

Life at Ismailia was like an armed camp. This sizable town was built by the British midway on the Suez Canal to control and service the passage of ships. It was still heavily populated by Egyptians, any one of whom might assist terrorists, or be a member of the Ikhwan himself. Movement in the canal zone was at a standstill. To send a truck anywhere with supplies meant having to send a patrol of armed vehicles, fore and aft, to protect it.

The bitter lesson of this was that Britain, for all its armed might, was unable to control the situation unless it carried through the struggle to its logical conclusion by reoccupying Egypt. The only other basis on which the British could remain in the canal zone was with the goodwill of the Egyptian people—and this they had never possessed.

## Unrest in Cairo

Something was bound to happen. That's what the bartender at the famous Long Bar in Old Shepheard's Hotel in Cairo was telling his customers on January 26, 1952. The bar was well known among journalists, both for the drinks (the bartender could mix anything) and for the tips that could be picked up. On this particular day, the bar's patrons had barely time to slip out the back way when the mob broke in, armed with crowbars, cans of gasoline, and long wicks with which they set fire to the curtains and draperies. Every bar and cinema, every haunt of the hated foreigners—all were gutted that day. The Canadian trade commissioner, J. M. Boyer, who was caught by surprise at the Turf Club, slipped away into the garden but returned to the building when he heard that an elderly woman had remained, locked in a cupboard. Trying to save her, he died in the flames.

All over Cairo, vengeance was wreaked that night—vengeance for a hundred years of exploitation, for a failure of human understanding between peoples of different cultures and beliefs, for all that Egypt had suffered since Rameses II lay dying at Per-Ramese while the foreign armies camped under the palace walls.

## Farouk Abdicates

On this night in 1952, another king of Egypt, Farouk I, trembled with fear. In the sumptuous but marble-cold halls of the Abdin Palace, he was faced with his reckoning. Having spent a fortune on nightclubs, women, and horses, he had lost the love of his people, who were fighting for their cause without him. Now he was blamed for everything—for the loss of the Arab-Israel War, for corruption in government, even for the death of the Supreme Guide, who had died in mysterious circumstances.

The government was paralyzed. The following summer, the king removed to Alexandria, to enjoy the cooling breezes along the Corniche. In Cairo, there were secret consultations among army officers to decide what should be done. A group known as the Free Officers Movement, already deeply infiltrated by Ikhwan and resentful of the death of their leader, had drawn up a plan of revolt. They presented it to Gen. Mohammed Neguib, and he accepted the nominal leadership of the movement.

On the night of July 22, 1952, army units moved out of their barracks and took up key positions in the city. The radio station, telegraph offices, police stations, government buildings—all were occupied without resistance. By 7 A.M., the Egyptian State Broadcasting Station announced that a new government, headed by General Neguib, would purge the country of "fools, traitors, and incompetents." The man who obviously filled all three categories was busy packing at the Ras-el-Tin Palace overlooking Alexandria's harbor. He had already given orders to have the royal yacht, *Mahroussa,* prepared for sailing. While negotiations with the army, whose tanks were surrounding the palace, continued, Farouk kept on stuffing trunks with gold and silver plate, with jewelry and Dior dresses belonging to Queen Narriman—anything that could be turned into cash abroad.

Then, at 6 P.M., Farouk emerged at the side door giving onto the landing stage. Resplendent in his white admiral's uniform, he shook hands with his aides (all of whom were left behind to face long prison sentences) and, stepping as nimbly as his exalted corpulence would allow into a launch, he and his family, including the heir, Prince Ahmed Fuad, were taken to the royal yacht. From the bridge, he bade farewell to Egypt with a last insouciant wave.

"Soon," the king had once said, "there will be only five kings left in the world; the Kings of Hearts, Diamonds, Spades, and Clubs—and the King of England." He had done his level best to fulfill his own prediction.

# The Rise of Nasser

## The Revolution

A young army officer who took part in the "night of the long knives" (July 22–23, 1952), looking back on the great event, wrote these lines:

> The pages of history are full of heroes who created for themselves roles of glorious valor which they played at decisive moments. Likewise the pages are full of heroic and glorious roles which never found heroes to perform them. It seems to me that in the Arab circle there is a role wandering in search of a hero. This role, exhausted by its wanderings, has at last settled down, tired and weary, near the borders of our country, and is beckoning us to move, to take up its lines, to put on its costume, since no one else is qualified to play it.

The young officer who cast himself in the role of hero was Col. Gamal Abdel Nasser. His name was utterly unknown to the world at large, but to the Free Officers Movement he was the moving spirit of the revolution. It was Colonel Nasser, not General Neguib, who sped around Cairo in his small Morris car on the day before the coup, leaving notes at the homes of his fellow officers; "It happens tonight. Rendezvous at Abdel Hakim Amer's at 11 P.M." It was he who masterminded the attack on General Headquarters in Cairo with no more than ten officers and eighty men—an attack that was unbelievably successful. It was he, not General Neguib, who directed the course of events after the abdication of the king.

*Gamal Abdel Nasser talking to the relatives of Egyptian soldiers taken prisoner in Israel during the Six-Day War.*

121

This young man of thirty-four, with his regular, heavy-set features, looked more like a Hollywood-type hero than a real-life revolutionary. In any other country, he would have been a young executive, a professional engineer, or a successful stockbroker. What made him choose revolution as his career? His father, a district postmaster in Alexandria, was able to give him a Western-style education. But, after one year at Cairo University, Gamal decided to enter military college.

Gamal Abdel Nasser was a young man on the make, and in Egypt the quickest road to success was in the army. But for him, as for many of his ambitious and somewhat naïve comrades, there were great humiliations in store. The Second World War proved the total subservience of Egypt to Britain, when British tanks surrounded the Abdin Palace and made the king a prisoner. Then came the Arab-Israel conflict of 1948. The Egyptian defeat was due to many causes, but the overriding factor, in the eyes of Nasser and his comrades, was the venal duplicity of the king. Egypt had to be cleansed, they thought, of the foreigners and their native stooges. But it is unlikely that Nasser or his friends had any clear idea of what was to follow. In his book, *Egypt's Liberation,* Nasser gives the following explanation:

Before the 23rd of July, I had imagined that the whole nation was ready and prepared, waiting for nothing but a vanguard to lead the charge against the battlements. Our role (that of the army) was to be the commando vanguard. I thought that this role would not take more than a few hours. Then immediately would come the sacred advance behind us of the serried ranks of marching feet. Then suddenly came the reality after July 23rd. Crowds did eventually come, and they came in endless droves—but how different is the reality from the dream. The masses that came were disunited, divided groups of stragglers. We set about seeking the views of leaders of opinion and the experience of those who were experienced. Every man we questioned had nothing to recommend except to kill someone else. If we had gone along with everyone we heard, we would have killed off all the people and torn down every idea, and there would have been nothing left for us to do but sit down among the corpses and ruins.

## Dreams and Disappointments

The Free Officers, having begun a revolution, found they had to go on and govern by themselves. Thus, their first move was to invite a well-known and respected officer, General Neguib, to assume the leadership. Mohammed Neguib, a gregarious upper-class officer, had no clear concept of the direction that should be taken. He called for free elections, but these were continuously postponed, as the officers feared to unleash anarchy on the land. Gradually it became clear that revolution meant undoing the harm of three millennia during which Egypt had been exploited. It meant abolishing the caste of landowners, who drew their titles and title deeds from the long years of foreign occupation. Orders went out to abolish titles such as pasha and bey. Landowners were permitted to keep one hundred feddans of land. Everything over one hundred feddans was to be distributed among the fellahin.

All this bewildered and alarmed Mohammed Neguib. As the only well-known figure among the revolutionaries, he counted on his popularity to sustain him when, in a dramatic announcement, he handed in his resignation. The resignation was accepted. No popular outcry came to his aid. And so, in 1954, General Neguib vanished from the stage of history into a private villa, where he still lives, virtually a prisoner under guard.

The future facing the revolutionary officers was truly intimidating. How were all these grandiose plans to be realized? Egypt had practically no engineers or technicians; extension of the arable land required a gigantic irrigation project equivalent to the largest dam ever built in the world; the only great national asset, the Suez Canal, with its huge annual revenue from the transit of ships, was owned by a foreign company. The situation of the Free Officers was desperate, and a gigantic effort was needed to sustain the revolution. But Nasser knew what to do.

Premier Nasser, as he was now styled, began with the dam. It would be costly, he was advised—at least $1300 million. It would take fifteen years to build. But if Nasser could build the dam, he would have a monument more immense even than the pyramids, and he would have saved the revolution. An initial approach to the World Bank was hopeful, but the bank made its loan conditional on Anglo-American support.

This support was, however, very problematical. Britain, which had been forced to sign an agreement to evacuate British troops from the Suez Canal by 1956, was not exactly an admirer of Nasser. The United States, frequently a strong ally of Israel, viewed with considerable distaste a loan of such size to Egypt, Israel's avowed enemy.

As if to exacerbate these Western prejudices and fears, Nasser proceeded at the same time to conclude a gigantic arms deal with the Soviet bloc. It was rumored that one hundred MIG fighters, fifty Ilyushin bombers, and three hundred tanks were on their way to Egypt. This upset the power balance in the Middle East. Grave questions were asked in Congress. In June, 1956, United States Secretary of State John Foster Dulles announced that the American offer of help to build the Aswan High Dam was off.

Perhaps Nasser knew what he was about, perhaps he didn't. But in any case his reaction to this news (after he had publicly thanked the United States for its offer) was entirely predictable. Like all his predecessors, he had been made a fool of in the eyes of his people by the Western powers. His fall had been forecast—and gleefully awaited in London.

The options open to him were few. Revenge was a tempting course, the only one, really, that would save him. And it was so easy. All he had to do was to seize control of the Suez Canal, that bugaboo of Egyptian politics for nearly a hundred years, and he could even the score. What is more, this would help to answer his dilemma by providing funds (from the tolls) for the High Dam. Egypt, he could say, would build her own dam. Whatever we think of Nasser, it would have taken a very high-minded and very brave man *not* to take this course.

## The Nationalization of the Suez Canal

Nevertheless, Nasser's announcement of the nationalization of the Suez Canal Company burst upon the world as an act of piracy almost without precedent. Given the background of distrust and enmity between the West and Egypt, it was easy for the Western press to build up the Egyptian ruler ("dictator" was the usual word now) into a monster of duplicity and evil. Nothing went wrong in the Middle East that could not be attributed to a "Nasser plot."

*A view of the Port Said harbor area, with the Suez Canal Administration in the center.*

Israel complained that Egypt was stirring up border raids by *fedayeen* (guerrillas) against Israeli farming settlements. This, of course, was quite true, although, in the context of raid and reprisal, which was habitual along the borders of the new Zionist state, it was not always easy to establish which was the raid and which was the reprisal.

The French were feeling the pinch of the nationalist Arab movement in French-ruled Algeria. French farmers were murdered in their beds. French police posts were wiped out, French leaders in Algiers were assassinated. Likewise, the British blamed Nasser for the activity of revolutionary Arab groups in other British dependencies, such as Jordan and Aden.

All this was quickly laid at Nasser's door. There is no doubt that he had lent encouragement to the Arab nationalist movement throughout the Middle East and Africa, but it is a misreading of history to suppose that these movements would not have taken place without him.

Nevertheless, Western governments tended to regard Nasser as the cause of all the unrest, and on this assumption they based their policies.

In Tel Aviv, in London, in Paris, the official line was that they had only to get rid of Nasser and all would be well. In fact, some thought a little extra push might be helpful.

## The Bombing of Port Said

Britain and France began toying with the idea of a joint invasion of Egypt. Sir Anthony Eden, the British Prime Minister at the time, was reluctant to undertake such an operation without a clear and undeniable justification. The French undertook to provide it.

The Israelis had already given the French notice of their intention to launch an even more punitive action than their earlier forays into Egyptian territory. The degree of collusion between the two governments may never be known. Some correspondents, like Merry and Serge Bromberger of the French magazine *Paris Match*, reported a secret meeting between the Israeli Prime Minister, David Ben-Gurion, and French officials at Villacoublay, near Paris, on October 22, 1956. What transpired at the meeting, if it ever took place, we do not know. But on October 29, Israel struck.

Within three days, Israeli forces had reached the Canal, having cut off the bulk of the Egyptian Army in the Sinai Desert. Hurried meetings took place between the British and French. The war, they agreed, must be stopped in order to save the Canal. The clear and undeniable justification had been provided. Britain and France would be the peacekeepers.

The methods of peacekeeping employed by the two Western powers are open to question. How did it happen that they had a large French-British force already in Cyprus *before* the Israelis invaded? Why did they demand that both Israeli and Egyptian forces should withdraw to positions ten miles from the Canal when this left the Israelis still one hundred miles inside Egypt? Why did they bombard Egyptian, but not Israeli airfields? And, above all, why did they launch an invasion *after* the two belligerents had accepted a cease-fire called for by the United Nations?

The answer given by critics of the Western powers is that the whole political drama, from the Israeli invasion to the French-British intervention, was a plan designed to overthrow the Egyptian dictator. If it was, it failed signally. Nasser himself had said that his greatest ally would be world opinion. And so it was.

126

From the first moment of the Israeli invasion, the United Nations Security Council was in continuous session. One of the most decisive agreements to come out of these meetings was the decision to send a United Nations peacekeeping force to the Middle East. Thus the last excuse for British and French intervention was removed. The Israelis were requested to retire to their frontiers, and President Nasser, who before the British-French invasion had been past help, was now secure in his position. Such are the ironies of history.

Meanwhile, the human drama was unrolling on Egyptian soil. On November 5—*after* the Egyptian-Israeli cease-fire—the Allied invasion began at Port Said. This city of 175,000 at the northern end of the Suez Canal was drowsing under its palm-shaded streets and squares, in the well-to-do European section with its spacious gardens and villas and the imposing administration offices of the Suez Canal Company, and in the Manach quarter, where forty thousand people lived in shanties built of lath and tin.

No one really expected the Allies to land. On the eve of this historic event, the terraces of the Casino were crowded as usual with people taking the evening air. The sidewalk cafés, their tables covered with white cloths and sparkling silver, did a roaring trade. Popular dance music played over the loudspeakers suspended along the esplanade.

At dawn, the Allied blow fell. The town was shaken by a tremendous naval and air bombardment. The compound of the Italian consul, Count Mareri, was filled with Europeans clamoring for admission. Mareri was known to have equipped his house with a bomb shelter and medical supplies. Driving through a hail of shrapnel, the consul made contact with the Allied commanders and the Egyptian governor, Mahmoud Riad, to try to arrange a cease-fire.

In another quarter of town the Russian consul, Anatoli Tchikov, was otherwise occupied. He was handing out rifles and submachine guns, which he had stockpiled for the occasion, to youngsters on their way to school. He then visited Colonel Rouchdi, chief of police and the right arm of Nasser, at Port Said. He must prevent a cease-fire at all costs, in order to provide the world newspapers and television screens with their maximum quota of Egyptian dead.

The Egyptian garrison consisted of only three thousand men, and no

*The Suez Canal in the days when it was a major international waterway. Since the war of 1967 it has been clogged with sunken shipping.*

reinforcements arrived. In the face of the massive Allied landing, the governor had no choice but to surrender. His decision was communicated to the Allied commanders. But then Col. Rouchdi arrived, with firsthand information that, before nightfall, both Paris and London would be wiped out by Soviet rockets. "We must hold on at all costs," said Rouchdi. Already the schoolchildren, armed with Czech *klashnikov* submachine guns, were in action.

And so, what Sir Anthony Eden and Mr. Pineau in faraway Europe had thought would be a simple, bloodless show of force, turned into a bloody holocaust in which perhaps as many as twelve thousand people died. Vast areas of the town were demolished and the Manach quarter was burned to the ground, leaving its forty thousand inhabitants homeless.

Already the Allied landing was behind schedule. "Advance the length of the Canal as soon as possible," was the order from Cyprus. It was

128

not until the night of the sixth, leaving a smoking town behind them, that the Allied forces were able to set out on their mission. Then it was too late. Condemned by the United Nations, under tremendous pressure from Washington, Britain and France had to call off their operation. The troops had not advanced more than ten kilometers along the Canal before they received the order to halt.

In a few days, the blue-helmeted United Nations police—Canadians, Finns, and others—arrived to take their place. Sadly, the British and French sailed away, all objectives lost. The Canal was filled with sunken ships (sent to the bottom by Colonel Rouchdi at the prompting of the ever-busy Tchikov). The Canal Company was still in the hands of the Egyptians. And President Nasser arrived in Port Said amid the frantic cheers of the populace as a conquering hero.

## The United Arab Republic

The effect of the short-lived war, therefore, was to give Nasser all he had asked for and more: victory, glory, and acclaim throughout the Arab world. From this point on, the Egyptian revolution entered on its expansionist phase. Of course, there always had been a growth factor in Nasser's calculations. It was called Pan-Arabism in the dialectic of the revolution, but the West called it imperialism. But it must always be remembered that the Arab people are accustomed to look on themselves as one nation, and the mantle of leadership had now fallen unequivocally on Egypt.

The first take-over occurred just two years later. But it was Nasser who was taken over! In January, 1958, the complete Cabinet of Syria arrived in Cairo aboard a plane to offer the accession of Syria to Egypt. This astounding event probably took Nasser as much by surprise as anyone.

Union between the two countries had been mooted for some time, but Nasser himself advised lengthy preparation. The two countries, although both Arab, were entirely different. Egyptians were slow and ponderous. Syrians were clever and volatile. Egyptian leaders were intensely nationalist but anti-Communist. Syrian politics had become a happy hunting ground for Marxist infiltrators. In Egypt, the fellahin were the most important part of the electorate. In Syria, the fast-talking merchants dominated the economy.

Events, however, have a way of taking their own course. The political scene in Syria had become so chaotic that the ruling Baath party feared an imminent Communist coup, and in order to avoid this, the entire government flew to Cairo to make a present of their country to the Egyptian dictator. Nasser had no choice but to accept.

The result was a new nation: the United Arab Republic. It included both Egypt and Syria, which were officially known as the Southern and Northern regions. Deputies from both countries sat in one parliament in Cairo (Syrian representation greatly exceeded what their numbers warranted). The former President of Syria, Shukri al-Kuwatli retired to Cairo with the title of Vice President. Meanwhile, twenty thousand Egyptian administrators swarmed over Syria, carrying out land reforms similar to Egypt's. Immediately, the Syrian landowners became hostile. When the banks were nationalized, the merchants moved their money to Beirut in neighboring Lebanon. It seemed as though the Egyptians couldn't do a thing right.

The showdown came in September, 1961. The Syrian Army staged another revolution and put Field Marshal Abdel-Hakim Amer (Nasser's chief coordinator for the Northern region) aboard a plane and sent him back to Cairo. The United Arab Republic was no longer united. Only the name has remained (it still stands officially for Egypt) to signify a broken dream.

Another attempt, also in 1958, to effect a similar union between Egypt and the distant dust-bowl country of Yemen, in the southwest corner of the Arabian peninsula, fared no better. Whatever the Arabs felt about the unity of their race and their cause, they could not agree on united leadership—not under Nasser nor anyone else.

Nasser had missed the tide, which, as Shakespeare says, if "taken at the flood, leads on to fortune . . . " This tide, which ran so strongly in Nasser's favor in 1956, had ebbed away, leaving him high and dry. Just how dry we were to discover in 1967 when, for the third time in twenty years, Israel and the Arabs engaged in open warfare.

## The Six-Day War

Once again, in the spring of that year, the air of the Middle East was electric with threat and counterthreat. The eastern frontiers of Israel echoed with gunfire as skirmishers from both sides invaded each other's territory. The situation was complicated by a new government in Syria, representing the extreme Marxist wing of the Baath party. The Syrians stepped up hit-and-run raids on Israeli farming settlements, and the Israelis replied in kind. On April 7, 1967, the Israeli air force downed six Syrian MIG fighters—over Syrian territory—the first use of aircraft in reprisal raids. And in May, the Israeli army moved up to the Syrian frontier in force, in response to widely broadcast threats and stepped-up border infiltration from Syria.

Nasser ordered the deployment of Egyptian troops along the Israeli border after he saw Syrian reconnaissance photos which showed Israeli troops massed on the Syrian-Israeli border. He then further complicated the escalating situation. He demanded (and got) the United Nations to withdraw its protective cordon of troops between Israel and Egypt. He began an arms buildup on the Israeli frontier. Then he closed the Straits of Tiran to Israeli shipping in the Gulf of Aqaba. There is no denying the provocation of these acts.

However, it must be remembered that the developments in the Middle East look quite different when viewed from New York, for instance, from the way they do when seen from, say, Port Said. From the Western viewpoint, the Middle East is a vast geographical area, split up into a crazy-quilt of bickering states, among which Israel is the smallest. Why not let the Israelis enjoy their little bit of land in peace, especially when they represent a people that has suffered wicked persecution in other parts of the world, a people whose roots in the Middle East go back several thousand years? This is the picture when seen from the West.

From the East, it all looks different. The Arabs feel that they have been the majority in the area since most of the Jews were expelled by the Emperor Titus in A.D. 70. They say that people can't just come back like that, two millennia later, notwithstanding their historical roots. As for the sufferings of the Jewish people, why should the Arabs pay for what Hitler did? So runs the argument in the East.

*Ismailia house damaged during the 1967 war.*

But behind this bitter feud lies an even deeper hostility. Westerners see Israel as a small state of three million Jews, which is fighting for its life against the goliath of sixty or eighty million Arabs. But Arabs see Israel as the long arm of Western imperialism—spreading over the Middle East, trying to take back all the territory that Arabs have struggled to liberate from their former oppressors.

It is against this background of opinion that Nasser's actions must be viewed. The demand for withdrawal of the United Nations police forces from Egypt was, in the Arab view, an act of courage—to show that Egypt, at least, was not afraid of Israel. There was nothing to prevent Israel from accepting the United Nations force on *its* side of the border. And if Israel had done so, neither side could have been attacked. But when United Nations Secretary General U Thant proposed it, Israel refused because it was felt that the police force would have stopped Israel, but not Egypt.

Similarly, in the Arab view, the closure of the Gulf of Aqaba was not a new act of piracy, but a reversion to ancient Arab rights. Less than three miles wide at its mouth, the Straits of Tiran, the waters of this narrow appendage of the Red Sea were wholly Arab until the seizure of the Port of Eilat by the Israelis in 1949. It was held by Israel in defiance of the United Nations armistice agreement, and it was the efforts of the United Nations mediator, Count Folke Bernadotte, to have Eilat returned to the Arabs that led to his assassination by Israeli terrorists.

Therefore, what seemed to the West a highly provocative attitude on the part of President Nasser won Egypt respect throughout the Arab world. Nasser's act was regarded as a courageous act of statesmanship; he was upholding the inalienable rights of the Arab nations. Yet he gave U Thant the assurance that he would not strike the first blow in an armed confrontation with Israel. Perhaps the Israelis had reason to doubt his word when they listened to the warlike threats on Cairo radio.

In any event, it was Israel that seized the advantage. On June 5, 1967, during the early morning hours of darkness, the bulk of the Egyptian air force was destroyed on the ground by Israeli air attacks. The Egyptian army, massed in Sinai, deprived of air cover, was completely demolished. The Israeli army, protected by its own air force, raced across the desert for the Canal. In forty-eight hours, the whole of Sinai was in Israeli hands; the blockade of the Gulf of Aqaba was smashed; and the Suez Canal was blocked from end to end with sunken ships. Egypt was totally defeated.

How could this happen? At once, the Egyptians sought an explanation that would exonerate them. President Nasser charged that British and United States planes had participated in the preemptive strike against Egypt. This caused great indignation in the West and is most likely to be untrue. Yet, while the fighting raged, the Western powers delayed the call for a cease-fire for two days with procedural matters in the United Nations Security Council. Nasser thereupon broke off diplomatic relations with the United States, and most Arab countries did the same.

By this device, Arab honor was saved. But it is not so easy to dispose of the blame like that. We must still ask the question: Why were Egyptian planes caught on the ground, with many of their pilots reported carousing in nightclubs in Cairo? The same thing had happened eighty-five years before, when the British caught the army of Colonel Arabi asleep in their tents at Tell-el-Kebir. The answer seems to be that the Egyptians cannot quite grasp the temper of the modern world. They confuse "right" with "might." Because they believe themselves clearly in the right, they do not see the necessity of defending their position. That is why, among other things, the Egyptian case is so badly told and so little known in the West. They indulge in much warlike talk, in the tradition of the old Arab *razzia,* or war of words, forgetting to maintain at the same time a twenty-four-hour alert.

In fact, the whole handling of the 1967 crisis was characteristically Egyptian. With the nation in ruins, the army defeated and in flight (a hundred thousand Egyptians left in the Sinai Desert without food or water under a midsummer sun), the Israelis in possession of the east bank of the Canal, President Nasser took to television to announce his resignation. With tears streaming down his face, he handed back his trust to the Egyptian people and then, in a response that is wholly Egyptian, they gave it back to him. "Gamal, Gamal, Gamal!" chanted the crowds of fellahin come into the capital. Nasser had won again.

The era of Nasser was soon to end. His health was failing, and in September, 1969, he suffered a heart attack. He went to the Soviet Union for medical treatment and doctors warned him against hard work. But events would not let him rest. The fighting that flared up in Jordan in 1970, between government forces and Palestine guerrillas, nearly split the Arab world apart. Everyone looked to President Nasser to heal the breach. He convened a meeting of Arab leaders in Cairo, during which he succeeded in bringing about an agreement between Jordan's King Hussein and the guerrilla leader Yasser Arafat. Nasser looked on happily as they shook hands. It was his last great act of statesmanship.

On September 29, 1970, President Nasser died of a heart attack. His

*In Port Said, young Egyptians happily hold up photographs of Colonel Nasser.*

image over the years had changed. From the firebrand he was in his early days in power, he had become a stabilizing influence in the Middle East. His passing marked the end of an era. He was succeeded by President Anwar el Sadat, who pledged to carry on his policies.

Nasser's dreams of Arab unity, which he had been unable to achieve himself, seemed much closer now that he was dead. On November 8, it was announced in Cairo that President Sadat had concluded several days of talks with Col. Muammar el Qaddafi of Libya and Maj. Gen. Jaafar Muhammad al Nimery of the Sudan, and that they had agreed to work toward a federation of their countries. An economic and political alliance between the three countries had existed since December of 1969. It was felt that they each would greatly benefit by a consolidation of their different economic assets—Libya's oil, the Sudan's potential agricultural resources, and Egypt's large and technologically more ad-

*President Nasser. This official photo shows him in a characteristic pose—proud, determined, modern in outlook.*

*The death of Nasser. Pakistani President Yehia Khan (far left) and Egypt's Anwar Sadat are covering the dead leader's tomb with a green silk cloth embroidered with Koranic verses in gold thread.*

vanced labor force. This union would result in a new nation of over two million square miles and containing more than fifty million people.

Less than three weeks later, Lieut. Gen. Hafez al Assad, the Syrian Premier and Defense Minister, met with President Sadat and declared his country's desire to join the Arab federation. Colonel Qaddafi and General Nimery have endorsed Syria's acceptance into the alliance, but after her past experience with a Syrian merger, Egypt is expected to move with caution in this direction.

The plans for the federation as a whole will proceed slowly, and no concrete union is expected to occur for several years.

# Modern Egypt

## A Life of Toil

But enough of history, war, politics. . . . These subjects live in books. It is time for you to seek again the real Egypt—in the green land of the Delta, among the brown mud-walled villages, where two thirds of the people are born and die. Here, under the eternal blue eye of heaven, everything seems timeless. The dust on the road rises in a haze, whitening the *berseem,* or clover, which is the ubiquitous green color of the countryside. In the dazzling brilliance you cannot see the people at first, but you can hear the unending squeak of the shaduf, the *saquia,* or the Archimedes' screw. Then suddenly you are upon them, thick as insects in the fields. Perhaps they are young people, combing through the cotton fields, looking for pests that threaten the harvest. During the growing season, whole schools are emptied of children, who search for the dark specks of the cotton-worm eggs on the underside of the leaves. They are paid ten piasters (twenty cents) a day for this work. Or people may be threshing wheat while standing on the ancient threshing floor in the center of the village, where the time-honored *norag* (threshing machine) separates the wheat from the chaff, and the winnowing is done—today as in the time of the Pharaohs—by tossing the grain into the wind.

Whatever they are about, the people are thick on the ground, for human labor is cheap, and every man, woman, and child has to justify existence by work. Yet, they would tell you, this is not work. It is life—life and work are one. No one is idle. No one has any holidays. Perhaps

*Construction apprentices plastering a wall in the courtyard of the Building Centre in Cairo.*

you will meet some young men and women who are visiting the village on their college vacation. But they are working too. They are part of a village service project. Their job is to study the needs of the village and train local people to carry out the program agreed upon. It may be no more than a clean-up campaign, or fixing the oil lamps in the village streets, or starting a reading class. From seven thirty in the morning to seven thirty at night, these young people fulfill their task, until they go back to school. In Egypt there is no rest.

## The Village Cooperative

There cannot be rest. A country with the densest population per square mile of cultivation in the world can survive only by endless toil. And even that is not enough. Planning was essential if the land was to be used economically for the greatest yield and with the highest financial return. The center of this planning is to be found today in nearly every village. Located in a clean, whitewashed building, enclosed by a small courtyard, it looks positively "American" among the jungle of mud-walled houses of the village street. This is the village Cooperative.

Step inside and meet some of the people who are changing the face of Egypt at the village level. The Cooperative committee meets several nights a week around a small trestle table in this house. On the wall hangs a sign that says in Arabic: "Cooperation will mobilize the human effort to solve the problems of rural Egypt." The meeting will be attended by the Cooperative secretary, usually the one man in the village who is literate, the agricultural engineer, who is an outsider, and the elected representative of the fellahin landowners. For each man owns his own land now, even if it is no more than half a feddan (the average is five feddans). The discussion may be about a system of crop rotation that will make it possible to unify the crazy patchwork of individual holdings into one or more manageable blocks of cultivation.

You may wonder what all the argument is about; the plan seems so simple and necessary. If every man grows his own crop to feed himself, there will not be enough food for everybody. But if all agree to grow a single crop—wheat, cotton, even potatoes for export (Egyptians do not

140

eat potatoes)—and the crop is marketed through the Cooperative, the income may be enough to feed the whole village. But opposition is strong. Egyptians are conservative, especially fellahin, and, as the visiting engineer may explain, "They think we are leading them toward communism." But in villages where the plan has been accepted, the results are good and the owners are still the owners of their own land.

All this seems simple enough. Yet for the fellahin it represents a revolution as earth-shaking as if the sun and moon left their courses and came to sit at their feet. Fifteen years after the revolution, one million feddans had been redistributed. A million and a half *tarahiel,* migrant workers, had been settled on their own land for the first time in history. And all this had been done by democratic processes, without killing anyone. Not for Egypt the class war of the Communist bloc, with its landlord trials and antisocial confessions and liquidation of "enemies of the people." Here, everything is done around the small trestle table in the Cooperative, agreed to by a show of hands of the elected representatives, and sealed with the impress of thumbprints on the plan of operation.

While the meeting is being held, there may be a game of Ping-Pong going on in the recreation room next door. "Look at the fellahin playing games!" quips the visiting engineer. (Fellahin used to be noted for their seriousness, considered to be too brutish for play.) In the dispensary, the veranda is crowded with pregnant mothers coming for prenatal care, by fellahin awaiting examination for eye troubles and bilharziasis. In another room, village women are taking sewing classes with machines supplied on the installment plan.

Of course, the greatest attraction in the evening is the new television set in the Cooperative clubhouse. In fact, the owners of the coffeehouses down the street are quite indignant about it—they're losing all their customers! But there's only one answer for that: Buy a TV set too! The programs may strike you as both familiar and unusual. Here is Perry Mason (with Arabic sound track dubbed in), a Cairo football match, a news program showing Israeli shelling of the Egyptian towns along the western bank of the Canal. But who is this turbaned figure on the screen, who holds the crowd spellbound by his endless talk?

It is a sheikh of the Azhar expounding the application of the Koran to the problems of everyday life. We may be in the TV age now, but the Koran still has all the answers.

In fact, the life of the whole village now revolves around the white-washed building on the main street. What had seemed to be a hopeless life for the people of the Nile Valley has been given a new vista. It is terrible to think what would have been the social upheavel if the Cooperatives had not provided a way out. But this is only a stop-gap measure. The real problem is still unresolved.

## Food from the Desert

And the problem is people. No matter how much is done to improve the standard of life, the problem grows faster than the solutions. In the first half of the twentieth century, the crop area of Egypt grew by one third, but the population doubled. There are many reasons for this. The average fellah's family is seven, and it is very difficult to convince him that he does not need so many children. His half feddan of land is insufficient for life; the more members in the family to earn a living, no matter how small, the better off they are. Or so he thinks.

No matter where you go in Egypt, you will hear the population problem talked about, but you will find no real answers. You may pay a visit, for instance, to the Ministry of Agriculture in Cairo. If you talk to a top officer like Dr. Said Nassar, he will tell you that more intensive cultivation of the Valley will provide food for many more mouths. With increased fertilizing the farmer is raising the productivity of the land. He is also diversifying crops in order to earn more on the export trade.

Dr. Nassar is developing a program to grow vegetables that can be airlifted to Western Europe during the wintertime. Britain now buys a large quantity of new potatoes in April and May. Beans and watermelons earn hard-currency marks in West Germany. Tomatoes are an important part of Egypt's exchange trade with Eastern Europe. "And," says the earnest young doctor, smiling optimistically, "with the increased water available from the Aswan Dam, it will be possible to farm all year round, raising two and even three crops a year on the same land."

Others have sought the answer in a heroic campaign to push the desert back and create more land for the people. Such a man is Magdy

*Dr. Said Nassar, agronomist at the Ministry of Agriculture in Cairo, believes Egypt can increase its food output but can never be self-sufficient.*

Hasenein. On the Desert Road between Cairo and Alexandria, you will pass a lush garden province, filled, as far as the eye can see, with long lines of green: spinach, beans, watermelons, orange groves, banana plantations, even gladioli growing to a height of four and a half feet! Yet all this was once desert—until Magdy Hasenein reclaimed it. One of the Free Officers who made the revolution, Major Hasenein had served in the desert as a soldier for eight years. He believed that, with the help of agriculturists, irrigation experts, and town planners, he could beat the desert. With President Nasser's backing, he did. The area chosen was a strip seventy miles long and eighteen miles wide, bordered by a canal from the Nile, by the railway, and the desert road.

Tahrir (Liberation) Province, as it is called, is a monument to what men can do if they will it. Already when I first saw it, three years after its inception, it was a going concern. The land was cleared. The fields were irrigated. The tiny saplings were thriving. But the cost was

*Nile water is being lifted by a series of buckets and levers. This system of irrigation has been in use for centuries.*

terrific—four hundred Egyptian pounds (approximately ten thousand American dollars) per acre to reclaim. And there were houses to build, streets to lay out, electricity to bring in. . . .

But this was the idea—to make a completely fresh start. Major Hasenein chose his settlers carefully. They had to be young and bright, good students at school, and married, but with not more than three children. Each family was given a modern home, complete with electricity and plumbing, furniture—even cooking utensils in the kitchen. And, in the bedroom cupboard, was a complete wardrobe of Western clothes for both the man and wife!

Today you may see what this experiment has led to. Visit the old Egyptian villages first; then see Tahrir Province. Om Saber, capital of the Province, is now a flourishing town. Modern buildings line the main street—stores, movie houses, administration buildings. The saplings have grown into splendid shade trees. There is a comfortable blend of old and new. The traditional galabiya it much in evidence—it seems that the farmer found his new shirt and trousers too uncomfortable for working. But the women have taken to the new print dresses, which are produced in Cairo factories.

Each farmer owns his own land (five feddans). But here, land ownership is less obsessive than in the old villages. The farmer is looking for better income, and this he can obtain through the high quality of his crops (mainly citrus) developed and marketed by the ever-present Cooperatives. These new-type fellahin have clearly broken with the old pattern of life. Their families are small, and their income is high for Egpyt—150 pounds, approximately $350 a year after payments on the land.

But a total answer to the population problem has not yet been found. The cost of this project was too high. Major Hasenein himself came under investigation for overspending and retired to become a Member of Parliament for a Cairo suburb. But Tahrir Province was something more than a show window, as journalists often called it. The new fellahin of Om Saber are the children of the future—an image of what Egypt could be one day, when the clouds of war and international mistrust have cleared away and we can see how much the revolution has benefited its people.

## Industry

If neither the intensification of agriculture nor the reclamation of land provides an over-all solution, the answer must be found in industry. In the village shops and in modern Cairo you will find a complete range of goods, including all the necessities and many luxuries, all bearing the stamp "Made in Egypt." Indeed, many a market merchant will welcome you with a flourish as he shows the wares on his shelves and announces proudly, "And nothing imported!"

After the revolution, the new regime had to build the new industrial base behind high tariff walls. That is to say, Egyptian-made products were protected by a policy of exclusion of imports. Even today in the streets of Cairo, it is easy to spot the black marketeers who sell foreign goods–anything from ballpoint pens to soap–strapped to the insides of their jackets. But these goods are no longer in such short supply, nor are the Egyptian products inferior.

In Upper Egypt, an Egyptian doctor was able to treat my son with Egyptian-made antibiotics and sulfa drugs. It is possible to get parts for Egyptian-made transistor radios produced in Ismailia. Egyptian textiles are being produced for the export market, and the shortage in the stores is attributed to the need for foreign currency.

But the growth of consumer goods depends in the long run on the development of the heavy industrial base. The first big blast furnace was lighted at Helwan in 1958, and another in 1960. The problem of erecting heavy industry in Egypt was formidable. All the materials had to be imported–even the coke to fire the furnace. Gradually, these deficiencies were overcome. The Russians installed equipment that made it possible to work with coal. It was hoped to use the local ligneous coal from an Egyptian coal mine in the Sinai Desert; this mine has now fallen into Israeli hands.

Gradually all these difficulties–except the last–have been overcome. Production at Helwan is now at capacity. All the nuts and bolts for other

*Chemical industries at Alexandria.*

factories are made more economically at home. New factory buildings can now be erected with Helwan steel, and first-class sheet metal is being produced.

What all this means to the lives of Egyptians, whose numbers are growing by geometric procession, is incalculable. The theory, of course, is that as more and more of the surplus population are drawn into industry, they will acquire a higher standard of living and a higher set of social demands. To realize these demands they will keep their families small, and so reduce the pressure on the nation's food supply. Eventually, say the optimists, Egyptians may import most of their food and supply the Middle East with manufactured goods, as England does.

## Education

To realize a dream like this—and it is still only a dream—the first requisite is a mass educational system geared to an industrial economy. Even day laborers need to know how to read to know safety regulations,

*Many village schools are still set up under trees along the Nile.*

and in a nation that is more than 50 percent illiterate, this creates a gigantic task. By 1965, 75 percent of the children up to twelve years of age were in primary school; soon, school attendance should be general. The tragedy is that less than 10 percent of primary schoolchildren go on to high school. To bridge this gap, perhaps by economic incentives to families who need the income, must be the next step.

Universities like Al Azhar in Cairo are crowded now with three times the enrollment in pre-revolutionary days. But the old-style Koranic education is no longer in demand. The emphasis in the new universities is on technical subjects. For instance, the new university of Upper Egypt at Assiut at first offered only courses in science, agriculture, veterinary studies, and medicine—leaving the arts till later. Many students who cannot master the sciences switch to arts subjects, thereby cluttering up the ministries in Cairo with supernumerary personnel—one of the penalties of a government policy that promises jobs to *all* graduates!

In education, as in industry, as in agriculture, everything is a gamble against time. Can the land be effectively reclaimed? Can the industrial

148

base be built fast enough to buy the food Egypt cannot produce? Can enough good students be produced to staff the new industries? Can all these things be done in time?

No one knows the answers. Perhaps all that matters is that, despite international misunderstanding, war, the armaments race, loss of the revenues from the Suez Canal, Egypt is still trying to beat the statistical time bomb—

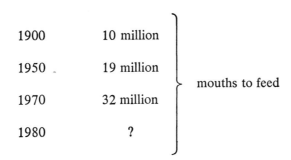

| 1900 | 10 million | |
|------|------------|---|
| 1950 | 19 million | mouths to feed |
| 1970 | 32 million | |
| 1980 | ? | |

## The Two Faces of Cairo

Egypt is not a country where anything should be taken at face value. If you visit Cairo and stay at one of the luxury hotels, you will get a completely false impression of the Egyptian standard of living. These deluxe bedroom suites, sumptuous dining halls, liveried doormen in tarbooshes and pantaloons are no more representative of Egypt than a Hollywood movie. The Egyptians who lived in this style are gone the way of the beys and pashas, and their place has been taken by the foreign tourists.

On the other hand, if you lose your guide and wander through the back streets, even directly behind the hotel, you will observe the most shocking poverty. Broken curbstones, streets littered with straw and filth, shops without windows or doors, tenement apartments lighted by a single bare bulb hanging from the ceiling . . . and everywhere people in threadbare, though usually clean, clothes. Yet this, too, does not tell the whole story. For these are people pulling themselves up by their boot straps: it was only last year that they left their mud-walled villages where doors, windows, and electricity were unknown. For them, this is the beginning of the Great Adventure.

*Back street, Cairo. Older Egyptian women wear black dresses and shawls at all times.*

*The Nile Hilton Hotel in Cario.*

For the key to understanding other peoples and nations is to place them in time—*their* time, not *our* time. Each people has its own cycle. The Egyptians have gone through many complete cycles in their history. For some peoples, the first period—of alimentation, of taking nourishment from the land—is long. Then comes the growth period, when the people develop skills, arts and crafts begin to flourish, and industries may develop. And finally, a people will reach maturity as its full potential is realized.

According to this scale, the modern Egyptians are just beginning to move from the first to the second period of development. It is quite misleading, therefore, to compare Egyptian life today with North American or European standards, which are already well into their third period. Rather, we should compare present-day Egypt with England of the early nineteenth century, or Russia of the early twentieth century. By these standards of comparison, Egypt has effected its transition from a feudal, agricultural economy to a primitive industrial society with a minimum of human cruelty and with much greater speed than either England or Russia.

Immense dislocations occur, of course. Cairo presents the appearance, at least in its main streets, of a twentieth-century metropolitan capital. Impressive boulevards, a mixture of colonial buildings, like the Cairo Museum, and modern pyramidal structures, like the TV building, create a misleading impression.

Most of the cars one sees are antique American models. Unfortunately, since the cutting off of American aid in 1967, there have been no spare parts available, and it is not unusual to see cars that literally are tied together with wire and string. It will be some time before the new Nasr, Egyptian-built cars, are available in any quantity (orders are two and a half years behind schedule).

As for the modern buildings, often only the façades are contemporary American. When you step inside, you pass back in time to an earlier epoch. Elevators either do not work or are nonexistent. The stairways are heaped with the dust of the khamsin wind, which blows through the glassless window frames.

In the ministries, the anterooms are filled with hordes of "clingers-on" in peasant galabiyas who wear out the leather on the ottomans while waiting for the "Great Man" to come out the green baize doors and dispense largess in the form of jobs and favors—a scene straight out of the Mameluke past.

And yet, despite these discrepancies, things do work. And one is aware of a readiness and a kindness on the part of these officials that is rarely seen in the West. So the phone line is not working to make your next appointment? *"Malish!"* (Don't worry.) "We'll go by car." No trouble is too great, no smiles are spared to make you feel at home.

This is the Egypt most foreigners and many correspondents miss. Often this is due to the immense misunderstandings that exist on both sides. Egyptian mistrust of the West is based on an exaggerated suspicion of "complicity" with Israel. While Western contempt for Egyptian "inefficiency," often based on mistaken premises, is all too seldom concealed.

Yet the gap is being bridged. As Egypt draws abreast of the industrial age, we shall come to see that, even with all their handicaps, the modern Egyptians know what they have to do and are capable of doing it. And they, in their turn, will discover that not all Westerners wish them ill or take pleasure in their defeats.

## *The National Assembly*

It would be easier for Westerners to appreciate what the Egyptians are doing for their country if they saw the National Assembly in action. One of the principal causes of misunderstanding is the Western notion that Egypt is a dictatorship. Technically, this may be true, although the President is freely elected. There is, however, only one party, the Arab Socialist Union. In the Western conception of things, this savors too much of totalitarianism. According to Egyptian ideas, however, a single party makes for order but does not stifle opposition.

Delegates to the Assembly are elected on a basis of at least 50 percent worker or peasant representation. Here is another arbitrary rule with an undemocratic flavor. But, any Egyptian will ask you, what is so democratic about a parliament made up of landowners and big-business men? The Egyptian way, the ordinary citizens are becoming accus-

*Egyptian Parliament.*

tomed to the business of legislation and government. Everyone remembers the chaos of representative government in the days of the Wafd, and no one wants it back. When the average Egyptian has learned the business of government, there will be time to try a full-fledged democracy.

Meanwhile, a visit to the Assembly certainly proves that the parliamentary opposition in Egypt is alive and kicking. The government may present legislation, but that does not mean it is automatically passed. If the issue is about women's rights, Delegate Fatma Diab is sure to be on her feet. A peasant herself, and owner of a three-feddan farm, she is a champion of legal rights for women, with equal pay for equal work. Her fiery oratory commands respect in the Assembly. Of the 360 elected members, 8 are women. Among the members are bus drivers, textile workers, professors, doctors, journalists, and the usual lawyers. It is a truly representative assembly.

And what happens if they reject government legislation? Then the bill is returned to the ministry proposing it, for modification or amendment in line with the criticism it has received on the floor of the House.

Thus amended, it may be presented again and probably will be passed. Everybody is happy—they have talked, they have argued, they have had their way. It is all very Egyptian, and it cannot really be called undemocratic.

## The Aswan High Dam

Another cause of misunderstanding with the West is the allegation that Egypt is a satellite of the Soviet Union. This is not true, for this is still a country where communism is not only forbidden but held in abhorrence by Koranic tradition. Nevertheless, much of the agricultural equipment for the Cooperatives and the industrial equipment at Helwan and elsewhere comes from Russia, and now there are Russian technicians in Egypt, and Soviet missiles guard the Canal. How is this to be explained?

In 1956, Egypt concluded several trade agreements with the Soviet bloc, under which Egyptian cotton was bartered, on a long-term basis, for arms and other manufactured products. This exchange was part of an over-all strategy of Egypt's leaders to play off the West against the East and so remain neutral and masters of their own destiny.

It is doubtful if it has worked out quite as it was intended. Egypt's principal crops have been mortgaged in exchange for equipment of questionable value, often unsuited to the country or the climate. Tractors have been known to rust unused for lack of parts to repair them with. New pumps sent from a Communist country to raise the waters of the Nile to the new irrigation channels seized up in the hot climate and would not work.

The principal test of the Soviet agreement has been the construction of the Aswan High Dam. This gigantic accomplishment has to be seen to be believed. And yet it is very hard to see. You must first obtain a civilian permit to enter the area, then a military permit, and even then you may catch no more than a glimpse. Photographs are absolutely forbidden. The reason for all this difficulty, however, is very obvious.

Everywhere surrounding the dam site are both stationary and mobile antiaircraft gun emplacements, manned on a round-the-clock-alert basis. For a country at war, the High Dam presents an almost indefen-

154

sible target. One bomb in the mammoth bastion holding back the waters above Aswan would devastate the entire populated country, sweep away villages, towns, and cities, and probably annihilate a majority of the population of 32 million. In fact, a country like Egypt, utterly dependent on this one resource, can really not afford to go to war.

It is part of the absurdity of the contemporary world that Egypt would build this vulnerable monument and still engage in hostilities with a neighbor. Yet, perhaps Egyptian thinking is no more illogical than ours. Armed to the teeth with nuclear weapons, we live in our all but defenseless cities, relying on the essential sanity of the "other side." In their heart of hearts, the Egyptians do not expect Israel to destroy the dam because of the effect on world opinion. But, by the same token, Egypt can never hope to annihilate Israel, since, in such circumstances, world opinion would hardly matter to the Israelis, and if

*Work in progress on the dismantling of the Great Temple of Abu Simbel. The statues were covered with sand to protect them while the stone over the temples was removed.*

they were on the brink of disaster, they might well bomb the dam. Hence, much of the war talk in the Middle East may be no more than highly charged bluff.

Yet, if you are to see the new Egypt, you must come to Aswan. Here, in one small town, past and present meet, and the future looms forth visible to the eye! From the terrace of the Old Cataract Hotel nothing much has changed. The wicker chairs are all still ranged in rows for the sickly tourists—mostly elderly Britishers—who like to come for their health during the winter months. The air at Aswan is the purest and driest in Egypt (also the hottest!). Below the hotel terrace, the land falls away to the river, among the curiously gnarled, black-red rocks of the vicinity. There, in the midst of the green water, is Elephantine Island, crowned now by a brand-new luxury hotel. But, alas!—the waiters at the Old Cataract can hardly contain their smiles as they tell you this—the new hotel is not open yet. "The war," they say, meaning the loss of the tourist trade.

Until 1960, Aswan was a sleepy town of 30,000. Now it is bursting its seams at 150,000. As soon as you take a cab and cruise the streets, you sense its frontier spirit. Houses and shops are going up faster than the streets are put in. The cause of all this boom is, of course, the dam. The nearer we get to the dam, the more we see of the boom town.

There are streets and streets of prefabricated Soviet-style workers' flats. And at once you are reminded that it was Russia that picked up the tab for the dam when America flung it down. That moment decisively influenced the shape of the future, and today Russian street signs can be seen everywhere. Russian workers and engineers are still at work on the site and huge painted propaganda displays show the Egyptian worker and the Russian worker clasping hands. Soviet news bulletins and party songs are heard on the car radio. All this does not mean that Egypt has gone Communist. It is part of the agreement under which Egypt and the Soviet Union jointly built the dam. But the world that has been created is a strangely Russian world, here in Upper Egypt, and it must have a strong influence on the young Egyptians who live there.

At the dam site itself, you will be ushered into a large display room where relief maps show the various stages of the dam's construction.

Your guide explains that the new dam controls the entire flow of the Nile from south to north. Consequently, a waterway was dug on the eastern bank of the Nile to divert this flow. This waterway consists of an upstream canal 1150 meters long and a downstream canal 485 meters long, leading to the twelve generating units of the power station. Each generating unit has a power of 180,000 kilowatts. The total power of the station is therefore 2,100,000 kilowatts. This energy will be transmitted to Cairo over two extra-high-voltage overhead transmission lines.

After listening to all these figures, you may feel a little dazed and seek enlightenment from the way it really looks on the ground. But you may not get very far. The police, ever watchful for spies, may not permit you to go close to the source of the roaring waters. It is a pity that suspicions and fears have so far poisoned international relations that these difficulties should arise.

But if Egypt's dream is fulfilled, if over a million acres of land are added to the cultivated area by new irrigation, if the new electric power trebles the industrial potential of this burgeoning land—the "new Egypt" will be born indeed. This Egypt, shorn of its old griefs and fears, will be a happier Egypt, an Egypt more self-assured and proud of its accomplishments once again, as it was proud of its ancient pyramids. In time to come, the High Dam at Aswan will be recognized as one of man's greatest technological achievements. It will be the pride of the people of Egypt to be able to say, "It is ours!"

# Interlude
# By Nile Steamer Through Nubia

The scene at Shellal is biblical. The whole geography of Lower Nubia above Aswan is torn and tumbled about as though the world were in the process of creation. There is no greenery, no habitation, no life of any sort. Instead, one sees only great whalebacks of black granite, boulders the size of hillocks lying about in profusion, hollows like moon craters everywhere. Why this tortured landscape? The answer itself is as old as the Old Testament: these were the quarries of the Pharaohs from which they hewed the granite for Karnak and On, and even for the Temple of Baal in faraway Palestine.

Down by the river at Shellal, life appears, boiling and frothing in a swirl of colored turbans, as an immense mob gathers around the jetty. The twice-weekly Nile steamer belonging to the Sudan Railways is about to leave. The world ends at Aswan; to go beyond, you must go as the Pharaohs went—by water. Everyone who has business in Nubia is here, therefore, buying passage at the ticket office, carrying his bundles aboard, shouting some last farewells from the rail.

The Nile steamers are a tradition of the British "pasha era" adapted to the needs of a modern society. Traditionally, there are three steamers lashed abreast, for first-, second-, and third-class passengers; they are preceded by a fourth steamer or tug, which takes the others in tow. First class consists of a cabin with three or four bunks shared indis-

*A river steamer at Juba in southern Sudan is filling up with tribesmen who have been recruited to work on the cotton fields of the Gezira.*

159

criminately. It is easy to see that these cabins once had all the Spartan luxury a British civil servant expected: a washbasin, a fan, an electric light—and privacy. All these amenities, alas, are casualties to the advance of democracy. The light no longer works, the fan is broken, there is no water in the tap, and no lock on the door. But instead there is a jolly community spirit, as everyone drifts in and out engaging in Sudanese or Egyptian card games, such as Basra and The Boy, on the floor.

The other classes aboard enjoy more primitive conditions. Each of the other barges consists of upper and lower decks, on which mats are unrolled and family groups gather around in circles—sleeping, talking, eating. These are mostly Sudanese families, going home after visits to relatives or attending weddings in Egypt.

A colorful and unexpected element on the third-class deck are the inevitable hippies, some from France, England, and Germany, many more from America. This has now become one of the regularly traveled "hippie routes" to India, that mecca of all who reject the twentieth century. Since the closure of the Suez Canal due to the war, and the difficulties of the overland routes through the Middle East, the hippie traffic now ascends the Nile and strikes across Nubia for Port Sudan, where ships are obtainable for the holy land of gurus and yoga.

On a recent trip aboard the Sudan steamer, I spent considerable time with the hippie contingent. Among them were a young Holly-wood producer, a black militant from St. Louis, a political-science graduate from Winnipeg. The first two had already adopted the gala-biya and skullcap of the Egyptians. They inveighed at great length against the Western way of life, its crassness and its abominations. "Here," they said, "we feel free." Their freedom, however, was purchased at the price of charity from others much less fortunate, and there was something disturbing in seeing these children of affluent America begging scraps of food from the humble tribesmen who had barely enough for themselves. Yet there was a strength of principle in their protest. I noticed that, hungry as he was, the ex-Hollywood producer refused to accept meat—he was following in the steps of Gandhi.

Every morning and every evening on the lower deck of the first-class

steamer, the Sudanese cook prepared a meal. First he filled a large caldron with water, drawn up in buckets from the Nile. This he placed on an antique iron stove, which he lighted with wood. While the fire caught, he placed his prayer mat on the iron deck and performed the morning or evening prayers, facing Mecca. When he had finished, he made meat patties and put them on to fry with rice and lots of oil, turning them occasionally, while he sat cross-legged on a stool reading aloud from the Koran.

This cook was a remarkable man. He had recently suffered a terrible burn on his leg, caused by boiling oil. The wound had been allowed to fester, and the leg was now in a pitiable condition. I gave him what ointments I had, but it was past superficial aid. Yet he never complained once, and went about his duties with stoical calm, without missing one *surah* of the Koran.

Meals were served on a table covered with a checked cloth, which was put on the open deck. The Captain usually joined us. He was a

161

weatherbeaten man who had been a sergeant in the Egyptian Army during British times, and for twenty years now was Master of a Nile steamer. We talked of the changes wrought by the revolution and the dam. It was easy to see he was a bit bewildered by both.

From his pocket he produced a timetable of the steamers in other days. It called for forty-two stops between Shellal and Wadi Halfa on the Sudan border. Not one of these stops exists anymore. The building of the High Dam has created a lake (named Lake Nasser, after the President) 250 miles long and an average of 6 miles wide, completely obliterating all the villages of the former Nile Valley above Aswan. But here and there, the Captain pointed out to me the minaret of a mosque, nine tenths submerged, still floating its crescent above the waters.

"But what has become of all the people?" I asked. The answer is that they have been moved, at least 150,000 of them, to new homes

*The railway platform at Atbara in the Sudan. The railway industry is one of the biggest employers in the Sudan.*

in the Nile Valley. Doubtless they are model homes compared with their old, perhaps even with modern, brand-new kitchen utensils and a new wardrobe in the cupboard. One hopes the new tenants are happy. But something precious has also been lost. The Captain said this submerged land was one of the most fertile and peaceful parts of the Nile, beautiful beyond comparison.

At Wadi Halfa, the strange trio of ships tied up at a temporary landing stage on the edge of the desert. The former wharf and all the town are now submerged. This is the port of entry into the Sudan, and the Sudanese officials boarded us to examine passports. Fortunately, I had previously arranged to be met by a car which took me eleven miles across the desert to the terminus of the rail line to Khartoum. The dozen hippies were not so lucky. Without money or transport facilities, they staggered across the sand under a noonday sun. Three fell and were abandoned on the way, to be picked up later. The Sudan railway let them ride an open flatcar without sides for two days and nights, in heavy sandstorms, so that they could reach the coast. Yet, I caught a last glimpse of them at a railway station platform in Atbara, where we had stopped briefly. The black militant from St. Louis, his galabiya girt about him and his hippie beads swinging from his neck, was holding forth on the evils of Western civilization to an enraptured crowd of black Sudanese students (all clad impeccably in Western slacks and starched white shirts). Here was a clash of cultures going in opposite directions.

"What do you make of him?" I asked one of the Sudanese students.

"We call him a vagabond," was the reply.

That was my last glimpse of the hippie contingent. I hope that in India they have found the peace and contentment they sought.

# PART II. THE SUDAN

# The Road to Omdurman

## A Land of Contrasts

When you enter the Sudan, you enter Africa. Of course, Egypt is *in* Africa, but it considers itself a part of the Middle East, with all its variables of climate, geography, and politics. The Sudan makes an altogether different impression on the traveler. This huge land of almost one million square miles overwhelms you with its size, its gigantic wastes, its pitiless sun, its stern, dark peoples, its fierce, primitive ardor. This, you cannot help feeling, is an African land, and in many ways the Sudan is the heart of Africa.

It consists of an immense basin bounded by highlands on the west, south, and east, and sloping gently toward the north. This basin carries the waters of its great rivers—the White Nile, the Blue Nile, and the Atbara, northward to Egypt. For this, if for no other reason, the destinies of these two countries have long been closely interwoven.

The White Nile, which rises in the tropical forests of central Africa, is tired and thin when it traverses the Sudan, but it is reinforced at Khartoum by the waters of the Blue Nile, which rises in Ethiopia. When the Nile reaches Egypt, 57 percent of its waters has been contributed by the Blue Nile, 14 percent by the Atbara, and only 29 percent by the White Nile.

The northern part of the country is desert, with rainfall ranging from none to about eight inches a year at Khartoum, and agriculture is possible only with the aid of irrigation along the banks of the great rivers.

*A view of a village just outside Kassala in the Sudan.*

*A Sudanese village in the northern part of the country.*

In the central part, rain-fed agriculture is feasible when supplemented by giant irrigation work such as the Gezira Scheme, which produces the cotton crop on which the economy of the country depends. In the south again, entirely different conditions prevail. Here, heavy rainfall has created lush tropical forests. The Sudan is, therefore, a land of immense contrasts and conflicts.

Seen from the window of a train, which is painfully wending its way across the lonely Nubian Desert, the immensity of it all appears a bit overwhelming. Who can live on these blinding sands, and how? you wonder. And then there appears, here and there, a settlement behind a lofty mud wall (black mud here, not the warm red mud of Egypt). Often only a single gateway opens in a wall a quarter of a mile long. Behind it wave a few scraggly palms, the only green to be seen in the desert. If the train mounts an embankment, the traveler may catch a glimpse of what is behind the wall: many narrow alleys, and rows and rows of flat-roofed houses, all exactly alike, and rather resembling a honeycomb. A single tribe lives here, with its many families, branches, and subdivisions. There are 597 tribes in the Sudan, comprising 56 tribal groups. The northern tribes are Arabic in origin, and probably call themselves Arabs, although they are darker in complexion than the Arabs of Arabia and the Middle East. In the south, you encounter an entirely different racial group, the so-called Nilotic tribes, who are "real" Africans.

The very names of the provinces of the Sudan conjure up impressions of this lonely grandeur: Kordofan in the center of the country and Darfur in the west are the nomad paradise. Out of these sandy wastes thunder the hooves of the camels, mounted by rifle-carrying, sun-blackened men, whose only law is the Law of Islam and who live by the Code of the Desert.

In the Bahr-el-Ghazal Province in the southwest live the Nilotic tribes, the tall Dinkas and the warlike Nuers, who live by cattle breeding. And

*Tribal dance. The Sudan is made up of a great many different tribes of Arab and Negro origin.*

in the South, in Equatoria, we find people that are related to the tribes of Ethiopia and Kenya.

How was such a diverse land created? The answer, as in most of the emerging independent nations of Africa, is to be found in the history of colonial conquest, which partitioned the continent in the nineteenth century. The Egyptians began their conquests of Kush (as the Pharaohs called the Sudan) as early as the third millennium B.C. More recently, Muhammad Ali, the self-appointed ruler of Egypt, annexed the Sudan in 1822. By that time, it had been settled by Arab sheiks, who traded heavily in slaves, bringing them from the interior of Africa and selling them to Egypt, Arabia, and the Middle East.

## The British Discover the Sudan

It was, in fact, the slave traffic that first attracted the attention of British explorers and missionaries to this region. Many of them were men and women of highly idealistic bent who deplored the slave trade and felt a religious call to put a stop to it. In their wake came the generals and armies, often dispatched to extricate the missionaries from the scrapes into which they got themselves. Thus, history is often made.

The courage of these intrepid travelers, one hundred years ago, amazes us today. As the train, traveling southward to Khartoum, follows the great bend of the Nile, you remember that in those days there was no railway. The only means of transport was by Nile steamer, perhaps a paddle wheel, which had to be beached at each of the six cataracts, disassembled, dragged over the sandbank, and reassembled above the cataract. In the desert still stand the crumbling remains of British forts, built for the protection of travelers. Nearby, the headstones of those who never returned are slowly vanishing beneath the shifting sands.

The first of the great governors of the Sudan, who defined the country's present borders, was Col. (later Gen.) Charles George Gordon. When he arrived on the scene in 1874, he was already a famous man, fresh from his exploits in the Crimea and China. Nor did he arrive at the head of a conquering army. He accepted the appointment from the khedive of Egypt, who still exercised nominal control over the coun-

*Nothing is sadder than the flimsy gravestones on the desert, soon to be covered up with sand.*

try. In actual fact, the Egyptian garrison never dared venture outside of Khartoum. In the great plains of the south and west, the native sheiks ruled autonomously, making fortunes out of the black slave traffic. General Gordon set himself to change all that.

And change it he did. He was an extraordinary man—small, dogged, with blazing blue eyes, who had superhuman energy and unfailing kindness and loyalty. He made the Sudan his private world. "No one can lift hand or foot in this land without me," he once said. Alone, he subdued the tribal chieftains, riding his camel day and night for months on end, making peace, striking the chains off slave gangs, remitting the taxes of the poor. Everywhere he was obeyed, not because of the strength of the poor Egyptian contingents he brought with him, but because of the strength of his personality.

Yet this could not last. A man like this, utterly selfless, idealistic sincere, such a man makes enemies. These enemies were former slave traders, Egyptian pashas who had grown fat on the land, Sudanese chieftains whose rule had been broken. They took their complaints to Cairo and tried to have Gordon recalled. The Khedive Ismael stood by him, but when Ismael fell from power in 1879 and sailed away in his yacht, Gordon's power was broken. He, too, retired to England.

## Gordon and the Mahdi

Yet it was not good-bye to the Sudan for good. A strange and terrible, oft-told story was in the making—one which modern Sudanese are deliberately erasing from their memories. It is the story of one man's stand against the jinn, or sand-devil, of the desert. The man was Gordon. The jinn, which was conjured out of the whirling standstorm during Gordon's absence in England, was the Mahdi. It may have been partly Gordon's fault for abandoning his work unfinished. Or it may have been due to the avarice and cruelty of the Egyptian governors who succeeded him. The ways of God, say the Arabs, are strange, and never were they stranger than then.

One day, news reached England of a revolt in the desert, that out of the blazing wastes of Kordofan had come a Mahdi, a successor of the Prophet Muhammad sent from Heaven to succor his people, so his followers believed. Everywhere, the Egyptian governors and garrisons were in flight. The Mahdi had "liberated" the Sudan. From an imperial point of view, this was not a good thing. If ragged tribesmen of the desert could send the foreigners in the Sudan packing, this might be a signal for risings in Egypt and elsewhere. Britain had just established her suzerainty over Egypt. Could she afford to let the Sudan go?

Gordon was sent for, more by popular demand than by settled government policy. Gladstone, the British Prime Minister, was very unsure of the wisdom of extending British power to cover all Egyptian possessions in Africa. In the end, Gordon was empowered to extricate the Egyptian garrisons and if possible make peace with the Mahdi. On January 18, 1884, he left by train from Victoria Station in London, with only a few shillings in his pocket, on one of the most heroic enterprises in British history.

Meanwhile, in El Obeid, the capital of Kordofan, the Mahdi sat smiling in his tent. The Mahdi always smiled, even when he gave the assent to executions, which were numerous in his camp. He was a smiler with a knife. The laws he promulgated were in keeping with the stringent code of Islam. He forbade all drinking and improper acts of the flesh; he adjured his followers to "adore God, hate not each other and assist each other to do good." The penalty for disobedience, even in the most trifling offenses, was flogging or death.

The Mahdists loved it. They cleaved to this severe faith with a fanaticism that matched that of their leader. The Mahdi was venerated like Muhammad himself. His bath water was gathered up in little bottles as a charm against evil. And his men firmly believed that to die in the service of the Mahdi was equivalent to a first-class ticket to Paradise.

## The Siege of Khartoum

In Khartoum, General Gordon was received with veneration of a different sort. He soon saw that these people—the more educated and civilized element of the Sudanese people—were fearfully afraid of the

*View of Khartoum, capital of the Sudan.*

Mahdi. To them he was Jinn, "the scourge of God." They implored Gordon to save them, putting all their faith in the Englishman with the blazing blue eyes.

Gordon was in a frightful predicament. His orders were to make peace with the Mahdi and evacuate the Sudan. Yet how could he desert these 34,000 people in Khartoum, who hailed him as their savior every time he appeared at a window? He sent emissaries offering peace to the Mahdi. In reply, the Mahdi sent him a jibba—the robe of a convert to Islam. Gordon threw it on the ground in disgust. He would never surrender, he said, and he would not leave.

There were in all, eight thousand soldiers in Khartoum—all Egyptian. The arsenal contained only ancient rifles, twelve pieces of artillery, and nine armed paddle steamers, which were able to keep open the lines of communication to Egypt. In March, the Mahdi, with an army of 30,000 men, laid the city under siege. Gordon could no longer leave. In faraway London, a reluctant Parliament authorized an expedition to save him.

Here were the makings of high tragedy. A British army of seven thousand men, under Gen. Garnet Wolseley, the victor of Tell-el-Kebir, set out up the Nile from Cairo on September 27. They made painfully slow progress. In this age of jet transport and parachute landings, it is hard to conceive the labor required to transport men, horses, cannon, and gunboats fifteen hundred miles into the desert. It took Wolseley four months to reach his destination.

Meanwhile, an incredible drama was unrolling in Khartoum. Gordon spent days and nights pacing the flat top roof of his palace. From here he could see the Mahdi's men slowly encroaching on the city's defenses day by day. He could also see his sentries manning their posts along the Blue Nile and on the landward side. They were always falling asleep, he complained, and he would have to send off runners to wake them up. He also had a telescope mounted on the roof, through which he watched daily for the appearance of the relief column to the north.

Food was running short in Khartoum. The merchants had sold their last sacks of grain, and the people took to eating rats and even the resin of trees. Gordon had to keep up their spirits with daily communiqués, promising the arrival of the expeditionary force within a week, in three days, in one day. . . . . Finally he would no longer receive callers at the palace. "They don't believe me any more!" He retired to his room alone and read the Bible.

All the while, the artillery of the Mahdi zeroed in on the palace. With the annual drying up of the Nile, the enemy across the river drew nearer.

> Tup-tup-tup [records Gordon in his journal], it comes into one's dreams, but after a few minutes one becomes more awake, and it is revealed to the brain that *one is in Khartoum.* The next query is, "Where is this tup-tupping going on?" A hope arises that it will go away. No, it goes on, and increases in intensity. The thought strikes one, "Have they enough ammunition?" (the excuse of bad soldiers). One exerts oneself. At last it is no use, one must get up, and go on to the roof of the palace; then telegrams, orders, swearing and cursing goes on till about 9 A.M.

People begged him not to light up the rooms of the palace, since they offered a good target for the enemy's bullets. When one Khartoum merchant, who survived the siege, made this protest, Gordon brought in a large lantern with twenty-four candles, placed it on a table in front of the window, and invited his guest to sit down with him at the table.

"Go, tell the people of Khartoum that Gordon fears nothing," he said, "for God has created him without fear."

But, in the privacy of his heart, he was giving up hope. On December 13, Gordon wrote:

> *Now mark this,* if the expeditionary force, and I ask no more than 200 men, does not come in ten days, the town may fall; and I have done my best for the honour of my country. Goodbye.

Yet the city did not fall in ten days, nor yet in a month. On January 25, Gordon was still playing the game. He summoned a town meeting and told the officials he had noticed a considerable movement of the Mahdist forces to the south, that is, the landward side of the town. He, therefore,

*Many handsome buildings can be seen along tree-lined Gordon Avenue in Khartoum. This is the entrance to the Office of the Council of Ministers.*

ordered every male from eight to old men to line the fortifications. In twenty-four hours, he said, the English would arrive. If he was disbelieved, he would open the gates. It was his last gamble. A witness noticed that his hair had turned a snowy white.

## The Death of Gordon

The following day—the twenty-sixth—the Mahdi gave the order to attack. In the early morning hours, this order sent fifty thousand Arabs wildly yelling through the defenses, running carelessly across the quarter mile of nails and broken glass placed in the sand as though they were possessed. No wild animals, survivors said, ever behaved as the Arabs did in that one short hour before dawn.

Gordon was awakened from his sleep. Still in his nightclothes, he went up on the roof, just in time to seize a gun and fire down on the crowds converging on the palace. When they were too close under the walls for him to be able to bring them within the range of the gun, he went

174

down again and put on his white uniform and sword. At the head of the stairs he waited for them. An Arab cried, "O cursed one, your hour has come!" Gordon made a gesture of contempt. Then he received the first spears in his body.

This same day, the expeditionary leaders realized that they would be unable to bring the full column through the Mahdi's lines without further delay. They decided, therefore, to send a flotilla of gunboats into Khartoum. As the convoy approached the outskirts of the city, Arabs called from the bank that they were too late; the city had fallen, and Gordon was dead.

The story has been told at this length because it is one of the great military stories of courage, and because it was a turning point in the history of the Sudan. The event means something different to the Sudanese than it does to Englishmen, and something else today than it did in Gordon's time. In Khartoum today, it is difficult to find any record of the battle. The palace, now the President's, is closed to all visitors. Photographs of the building are strictly forbidden. No one can remember where on the stairs Gordon fell. For the Sudanese, the subject is closed.

In Western countries, likewise, it is now fashionable to decry the whole episode as a piece of stubborn imperialism. Gordon's intervention in the Sudan is argued in much the same way as the American intervention in Vietnam in the 1960's. Some say he had no business in the Sudan, and the Sudanese should have been left to work out their own destiny. Others say he was fighting for the Empire against barbarism.

Such arguments are stereotypes. They do not take account of the man. From his journals, it is clear that Gordon died for honor, not for the Empire. He was no imperialist. His relief came too late because Britain's rulers dragged their feet in their reluctance to become involved in a far-away country. It was Gordon's heroism, his refusal to cut and run, that *forced* Britain to assume the imperial role.

## Mahdist Sudan

Meanwhile, the British retired and the Mahdi held the field. From far and near, the laggard tribes came in to present their fealty to him. He ruled over an area half the size of Europe. It was a land of fear and mystery, from which no word was ever allowed to escape. After the fall of Khartoum and a massacre of the inhabitants in which at least four thousand people lost their lives, the Mahdi evacuated the city and retired across the river to Omdurman. Here he held court like a great oriental despot, and Omdurman, which had been an unimportant village up to that time, quickly developed into a bustling city.

Gone now were all the injunctions against wealth, ease, and the sins of the flesh. The Mahdi built a palace in which he gave himself up to every kind of pleasure. Surrounded by his harem, clad in the richest clothes, he ate and drank until his bloated body could stand no more. Only five months after Gordon's death, the Mahdi too passed away— from self-indulgence. His memory has been venerated ever since. An enormous tomb, eighty feet high, was built over his resting place. Pilgrims came from all over the Sudan to pray at the grave. It was believed to be a holier thing to do than go to Mecca. Even today, the Mahdi's family is one of the most important in the Sudan, and his descendants are among its richest and most powerful people.

The Mahdi was succeeded by the khalifa Abdullah. He was a ruthless man who ruled by terror. Slavery, of course, was reestablished, and over a thousand slaves worked on the khalifa's personal estates. He had a bodyguard of five hundred men and a harem of four hundred women. People coming in to see him had to crawl on all fours, looking at the ground. The jails were bursting with prisoners, for the khalifa grew wealthy from the confiscation of properties.

Gradually, the country became depopulated. It is estimated that out of the original nine million inhabitants, 75 percent were exterminated during the khalifa's rule. One after another, a few tattered scarecrows made their way to the outside world, among them Rudolf Slatin, one of Gordon's lieutenants, who had saved his life by becoming a Moslem. His story, on which much of what we know of Mahdist Sudan is based, awakened Britain. The Anti-Slavery Society took to the soap box and the pulpit, and in 1896 a new crusade was undertaken.

## The Battle of Omdurman

The times had changed, and the British were persuaded to carry the torch of civilization to the distant corners of the world. A new expeditionary force was raised, commanded by Lord Kitchener, and enlisting in its ranks a young man by the name of Winston Churchill.

The expedition took two years to ascend the Nile and strike across the desert. In April, 1898, the first resistance was encountered at Atbara, where the Emir Mahmoud, one of the bravest of the khalifa's generals, made a stand with two thousand men. The Arabs were wiped out by Kitchener's modern artillery, and the emir was led away in chains. Churchill relates that after the battle Kitchener "rode along the line, and the British brigades raising their helmets on the dark, smeared bayonets cheered him in all the loud enthusiasm of successful war."

It was September when the British sighted Omdurman, surrounded by what seemed to be a "zeriba," a defense work of thorns and trees. Churchill described the scene.

> Suddenly the whole black line which seemed to be the zeriba began to move. It was made of men, not bushes. Behind it other immense masses and lines of men appeared over the crest; and while we watched, amazed by the wonder of the sight, the whole face of the slope beneath became black with swarming savages.
> —from *The River War* by Winston Churchill

The British expeditionary force, composed of British, Egyptian, and Sudanese units, was approximately twenty thousand strong. They faced an enemy more than twice that size. But here the technical advances of modern warfare tipped the scales against the khalifa. The power and range of the British artillery smashed the Mahdist advance before it ever came within range of the British troops. One eyewitness said, "It was not a battle but an execution."

The Battle of Omdurman was over in about three hours. British casualties were approximately four hundred. On the desert before them lay some ten thousand bodies of the khalifa's men. They died bravely, facing impossible odds—the fifteenth century versus the twentieth. The remainder streamed back into Omdurman, among them the khalifa himself, who stopped just long enough to pray at the Mahdi's tomb. Then, mounted on a donkey, he made his way out of town toward the desert of Kordofan, whence, eighteen years before, the Mahdi's revolt had arisen.

In Khartoum there was wild exultation. The hostility between the town-bred Arabs and the desert Arabs of the Mahdi was still latent. Kitchener was welcomed as a liberator. And in the palace grounds, a solemn ceremony took place. Before the assembled troops, a funeral service was held for Gordon. His body was never found, but the band played his favorite hymn, "Abide with Me," and the old gunboats fired a salvo in salute from the river. Kitchener had a subaltern dismiss the parade. He retired to the garden, overcome with tears. In faraway London, the queen wrote in her diary, "Surely he is avenged."

It was a year before the khalifa was caught. He made his last stand at El Obeid, the Mahdi's early capital. It was another unequal contest between a primitive and a technological society. The British attacked with camel corps and machine guns. The khalifa's soldiers held their ground like men of wood. When the day was lost for them, the khalifa and his emirs dismounted from their horses, and sat on the ground in a group to meet their death. There was no surrender.

In his report on this event, Lord Kitchener wrote: "The country has at last been finally relieved of the military tyranny which started in a movement of wild religious fanaticism upward of nineteen years ago. Mahdism is now a thing of the past, and I hope a brighter era has now opened for the Sudan."

Certainly the new century dawned with hope in a land that was wearied of lust and cruelty. The telegraph was at once restored. The railway built by Kitchener's expeditionary force brought the industrial revolution direct to Khartoum. Within a year, the River Nile was cleared and opened up to steamers all the way through the south to Lake Victoria.

Yet, the Sudanese do not regard things that way. Maltreated, oppressed, terrorized as they were under the khalifa's rule, nevertheless it was their own government. There was no flight of refugees from the Sudan even during the height of the Mahdist terror. If the British had not intervened, the khalifa would undoubtedly have continued to rule, until, probably much later, the Sudanese people brought in their own reforms.

Greatly respected as Gordon was in his day, the modern Sudanese have turned their backs on him. The statue erected in his honor in

Khartoum by Kitchener has been sent back to England. On the other hand, the Mahdi's tomb has been repaired, with fresh gold leaf glinting on its roof in the sun.

The khalifa's house in Omdurman is now a place of pilgrimage. Here are the gun emplacements from the decks of the paddle steamers that ran under fire during Kitchener's advance on Khartoum. Here is Gordon's telescope, with which he watched in vain on the roof of the palace for reinforcements that arrived too late. And on the wall are the yellowing maps of the Battle of Omdurman at each of the crucial stages of the fighting. But the crowds of Sudanese—old women in white robes and shawls, camel drivers in turbans, serious young students in spectacles—what they all come to see are the clothes the khalifa wore; the bath he used, like a small swimming pool with steps in it; the spears with which the Sudanese troops faced Kitchener's machine guns. In the battle for the minds of men, the Mahdi won in the end.

## The Black Sultan

The Sultanate of Darfur in the west was an ancient Arab kingdom which came into being in the sixteenth century. Under its sultan, Ali Dinar, who came of a line sometimes referred to as the "Black Sultans," Darfur became a slave state along the lines of Mahdist Sudan. Officials of the Sudan government, the nominal suzerain, were excluded from Darfur. This went on until May of 1916, when General Wingate decided to march on Ali Dinwar's capital El Fasher. The sultan fled, leaving behind his ancestral home, which was said to be one of the most beautiful works of Arab art in the Sudan, resplendent with parks, fountains, and pleasure palaces reserved for the autocrat. The sultan was captured six months later and killed.

# British Rule in the Sudan

## Khartoum

The sky is a cerulean blue without any hint of a cloud, except for the heat haze that whitens toward the horizon; the unbroken expanse of red-brown sand rolls on endlessly on every side; nowhere is there a shadow of shade to rest the eye or protect the body from the pitiless sun—until you reach the confluence of the two Niles at Khartoum.

Here, in an oasis of green, the British built their new capital on the ruins of the old. The Mahdi had destroyed the old Egyptian-built city when his men captured it from Gordon in 1885. They had abandoned it and retired to Omdurman across the river. Only scrub and sand greeted the eyes of Kitchener when he entered it in 1898, an eerie sight in the silent, crumbling streets littered with rubble—and here and there the skeletons of citizens who had died trying to reach the safety of the river.

Immediately, in sound, imperial fashion, Kitchener gave the order for the site to be cleared and a new city to be laid out, a city of broad boulevards in the shape of a Union Jack, converging at the center. Brick kilns were erected and houses immediately went up, good, solid British-style houses, all bricks and mortar, with shaded balconies, shutters, and gardens.

And that is the Khartoum you see today, with its impressive administrative buildings, arcaded shops, modern street lights, angle parking

*The cattle market at Kassala, Sudan. The men with the turbans belong to the nomadic Zebeida tribe, which raises camels for the market.*

for cars, and endless rows of air-conditioning units stuck in the windows along the main thoroughfares. But this cosmopolitan atmosphere is only superficial. Turn off into any side street and you soon find yourself on a dirt lane faced by mud-brick walls, an archway framing a wooden door, and above a balcony shaded by roller blinds. Watch out, or some unseen person may empty a bowl of slops on you as you go by! For there are no sewers in this city of 179,000. "Night soil" (a polite word for excreta) is collected every day in camel-drawn carts. The houses do not even have numbers, and postal distribution is a relatively new thing.

Khartoum is a facade—an imposing imperial facade fronting a noble but for the most part still primitive land, its people living in a nomadic or patriarchal stage of development. It is a tribute to the Empire builders that they built so well and created a working model of what the future might be before turning it over to the Sudanese to develop as they chose.

## Atbara

Provincial towns illustrate better the natural rhythm of life in this high desert land. Atbara, in the north, represents the industrial hub. It is a key point of the Sudan railways, the country's biggest industry. They were brought here by the British pioneers, first to supply the army of Kitchener advancing on Omdurman, later shooting out "feeders" to service El Obeid in the west, Khartoum in the center, and Port Sudan in the east. Roads have proved impracticable in desert country, so the life blood of the nation runs on rails.

So, as you might expect, you find a town of 35,000 clustered around the giant railway yards and manufacturing works of Atbara. Coaches and wagons are made here; locomotives used to be imported from Britain, but now some shiny new diesels from Czechoslovakia have made their appearance. About twenty thousand Sudanese work for the railroad, but their houses are very modest; the average pay for an engine driver is about thirty dollars a month, perhaps double for a clerk. No wonder so many (often well-educated people who speak good English) sidle up to you and inquire about the chances for emigrating abroad.

## El Obeid

El Obeid, at the western end of the rail line, is a reminder of the old Sudan, when it was the Mahdi's capital: a town of 65,000 still living by camel trading (a camel is worth sixty dollars) and bargaining in the *souks*, or marketplaces. It is a town of squat mud-brick houses, baking under an eternal sun on the desert steppe of Kordofan. What the British have brought here is to be seen in the railway station, the water-filtration plant (the water is sold, duly chlorinated, for one cent a four-gallon can), and the intermediate school. Sudanese students are smart-looking boys and girls, and you only wish there were more of them —but, until lately, there were only 25,000 attending intermediate school in the whole country, and only six regular high schools were in existence.

## Port Sudan

Port Sudan (population 45,000) in the east is, on the other hand, a solidly British town. It was wholly built to order by the British about 1910 and embodies most of the features and idiosyncracies of solid

*Freighters being loaded in Port Sudan, the country's major shipping center.*

*Crossing a Nile tributary by ferry at Wau in Bahr el Ghazal Province. The youth on the left carries a leather pouch filled with good-luck charms around his neck.*

Edwardian architecture: the bank, the church, the wharves and marshaling yards, all pay tribute to British taste and engineering. And an excellent port it is, annually funneling out about a quarter of a million tons of goods (mostly cotton bales) and taking in a third of a million tons (mostly textiles, petroleum products, and machinery).

## Pax Britannica in the Jungle

The towns of the south—Juba, Yei, and Wau—tell another story in which the British role is no less significant but altogether different. This is jungle country, where the houses are built of grass, conical fashion, with concrete sides for important buildings—the more concrete, the more important the structure is. These people are Negroid and live by their ancient laws, their customs unchanged. The British brought them Christianity, medicine, and schools, but the natives of Equatoria Province have continued their tribal existence, planting their corn in the rainy season and herding their cattle. Only in one important respect did the British change their lives. Before the occupation, Equatoria was a land of fear—fear of the slavers out of the north who frequently depopulated the countryside. When the British came, this age-old fear subsided. The Pax Britannica was felt and respected even in the jungles of Equatoria.

The men who made these changes and built the modern Sudan were a special breed. It is fashionable today to laugh at the image of the early British colonizer, in his sunhelmet and shorts, dispensing justice to the "lesser breeds without the law," traveling vast distances alone, getting up at dawn, dressing for dinner at night, always quite sure he knew what was for the best. Yet these men simply did their duty, giving their lives to a foreign land for little in return except a pension in some small British town, far from the sunlight and romance they loved. For they were, at heart, romantics, these administrators who brought peace, order, and the rudiments of what they believed to be the higher ideals of life to a land that had known none of these things. Perhaps someday they will be given their due.

## Sir Reginald Wingate

The first Englishman to set his stamp on the Sudan was Sir Reginald Wingate, who became governor general in 1899. He was the officer in charge of the force that hunted down and killed the khalifa. But revenge was not part of his makeup. At once he set to work to reestablish public security. A country in which a woman was able to go unescorted to the well, where an unarmed man could travel two thousand miles across open desert, where police were obeyed and criminals punished and where the law was above bribe—that was what Wingate wanted to create. And he did, and with only a minimum of staff and force.

His first lieutenant was Rudolf Slatin, that same "Slatin Pasha" who served under Gordon and who survived twelve horrible years shackled as a slave of the khalifa. Slatin became inspector general of the Sudan. After all, he knew the country like the palm of his hand and everyone in it. He set up an administration initially run by soldiers but later taken over by district commissioners to the total number of 140. The idea of a country the size of the Sudan being run by 140 Britishers, often working alone, in areas hundreds of miles from any armed support, must give some idea of the rectitude of these men and the respect in which they were held.

## Progress

The work of the district commissioners was often unprepossessing in the extreme. Setting up and enforcing regulations for sanitation, creation of village hospitals and clinics, and prosecution of a vaccination campaign—none of these things is initially very popular. Yet so effective were the results that the battle against malaria, bilharziasis, cerebrospinal meningitis, yellow fever, and sleeping sickness was soon all but won.

Then came education. Before British rule, the only schooling in the Sudan was at the feet of the sheik in the mosque. Now, elementary schools were set up in every province. Britain was later accused of going slow on lower education, although it might be argued that anything was better than nothing at all. But higher education was certainly not neglected. Hardly was the Battle of Omdurman won than Lord Kitchener himself set about raising the money in Britain to launch a full-fledged university, Gordon College (now Khartoum University). His idea was to staff the civil service with educated Sudanese.

Sudanization of the Sudan government was an early aim of British rule. It was, in fact, largely accomplished, although not entirely to the satisfaction of those Sudanese who later took over the country. Due to the scarcity of British officials, it was always necessary to fall back on "indirect rule," that is, local government by the Sudanese themselves. The whole complaint was that the British chose just those elements of society that seemed to the educated classes "backward"—the illiterate village sheikhs. Sometimes it was said that the British were turning back the clock.

## The Gezira Scheme

Yet anyone with his eyes open would have to see that progress was being made in the Sudan under British rule. You have only to take a car and drive southward from Khartoum into that vast triangle of land called the Gezira, between the two Niles. As soon as you leave town, you are axle-deep in desert sand. This is all there was here before the twentieth century. But early British engineers noted a useful geographical fact: a regular, gentle slope exists in the land from the Blue Nile down to the

186

*The Gezira is the center of Sudan's cotton economy and the site of one of the world's great irrigation projects.*

White Nile. This meant that a storage dam on the Blue Nile could be used to irrigate all the vast area of two million square acres, letting the water percolate across the triangle by gravity. The land is impermeable clay, so it was not even necessary to build tile conduits; ordinary ditches would do instead.

And so today, before you have gone very far, you find yourself driving over a flat plain, like the bed of a dried-up lake. If it is early in the season, it will be springing green with endless waves of cotton crops. Cotton is the white gold that is mined here, a crop of such gigantic proportions—over 600,000 bales for export annually—that it literally feeds and clothes the Sudan. In this sense, the Gezira *is* the Sudan, and it owes its origin to British engineering.

The dam was built at Sennar on the Blue Nile in 1925, at a cost of $30 million, with a further $35 million for the canals and subsidiary irrigation. A whole town was built at Sennar for the engineers and employees, and today these leafy avenues, lined with British-style bungalows, a clubhouse and swimming pool, have grown into a fine town site. Today more thought is being given to building the kind of modern

*View of the construction site of the Roseires Dam in southern Sudan. The ten-mile-long dam will store enough water to irrigate 900,000 acres of land in the Gezira.*

dwelling the Sudanese employees, the "water-office clerks," would want. Sudanese houses are built on a plan reminiscent of the tribal villages seen from the train window. There are profound social reasons for this. The home must contain an open area, the compound. Washing is done out of doors, domestic animals are kept there, and besides, in the hot season, the whole family will want to sleep in the open. The house is also divided into men's and women's quarters, for the sexes never mingle socially in the Sudan. The husband will entertain his men friends on the veranda in the evening; the women keep to themselves in the women's area. Yet these new houses are spacious and clean, many with running water and showers. This only goes to show that modernity can take many forms.

Out in the cotton fields, tenancies are restricted to forty acres each. The tenant is required to till his fields in rotation: cotton, grain and fodder. The water is free, and the profit is split—60 percent goes to the government, and 40 percent to the farmer. Most farmers make a prosperous living by Sudanese standards—an average $2,400 a year, but many tenants have acquired expensive tastes, with a tendency to buy cars and gadgets beyond their means. This is a prosperity they owe to the British.

## The Anglo-Egyptian Condominium

All across the country, in the years after Omdurman, the foundations of a modern nation were being laid. Everywhere dams, water borings, and artificial water tanks enabled the cattlemen to make the best use of grazing. The country gradually became erosion-conscious and a special Department of Land Use and Rural Water Development was set up in each province.

Nevertheless, a gap grew between the British and the Sudanese that resulted in several open crises. As often happens when a people move from a primitive stage of development to a more advanced level, they feel a resentment against the hand that aids them. Dark suspicions

*Sudan Gezira Board, Social Development Department: Clean milking at Barakat Boys' Training Farm.*

abound that the pace of development is too slow, that their condition is being "exploited," that somehow they have been imposed upon.

Specifically, the Sudanese complaints centered around the belief that the government was hoarding when they should have been spending. It is true that the British made the Sudan pay for its own progress. Educated Sudanese noted that there was no real attempt to develop national resources, to find oil, to locate minerals. A myth grew up that if it were not for the British, the Sudan would be one of the world's wealthiest nations, like Saudi Arabia, across the Red Sea. The policy of Sudanization was condemned as just a facade because, although six out of seven in the civil service were Sudanese, the remaining British seventh had all the power, prestige, and wealth. The standoffish attitude of British officials was resented, as were their houses along the waterfront at Khartoum, their exclusive clubs, and their sacrosanct womenfolk. No British woman, during British rule, was ever allowed to perform in a nightclub before an audience of Sudanese.

The situation was also complicated by the presence of Egyptian officials in the government. The justification for this goes back to Gordon's time. It must be remembered that Gordon had received his office as governor general from the khedive of Egypt, not from Britain. Lord Kitchener's conquest of the Sudan was, theoretically, to uphold Egypt's claim to sovereignty. Consequently, the government that was set up after Omdurman was called a condominium; it was divided between Britain and Egypt. In actual fact, Egypt had no say in the government, but nevertheless, many Egyptians who were stationed in the Sudan attracted a political movement around them. As Egypt became more nationalist, the Egyptian faction in the Sudan became a center for Sudanese nationalism.

In the twenties, a White Flag Society was formed in Khartoum to work for unity of the Nile Valley, in collaboration with an Egyptian League for the Defence of the Sudan. When Sir Lee Stack, commander in chief of the Egyptian Army, was assassinated in the streets of Cairo, a pro-Egyptian rising took place in Khartoum. Two platoons of the 11th Sudanese Battalion mutinied and marched on the palace. They were ordered to return to barracks, and when they refused to do so, the

British opened fire. The Sudanese took refuge in a military hospital, where they died heroically, resisting to the last man.

The pro-Egyptian element found its leader in Sayed Ali Mirghani, sheik of the tribes east of the Nile. These were people who had opposed the Mahdi's claim to power and allied themselves with the Egyptian cause. In those days they had supported Britain. Now they undermined British rule. Sayed Ali was a clever little man, the religious leader of the Orthodox Moslems and one of the two great leaders the Sudan has produced.

The other great sheik was Sayed Abdel Rahman, son of the Mahdi himself. In their surprising fashion, the British allowed this dynamic man to return to his father's estates on Abba Island and there to build up the wealthiest estate in the country. As leader of the Mahdist Moslems (that is, those who accepted the Mahdi as a reincarnation of the Prophet), Sayed Abdel Rahman was given the same veneration by his people west of the Nile as the Mahdi himself had enjoyed. Even the water in which he washed his hands was saved to be drunk by the faithful. And, with the curious irony of history, this Sayed grew into an ardent supporter of Britain. He strongly opposed the Egyptian claim, and when independence came to be discussed he would hear only of a free Sudan within the British Commonwealth.

The vendetta between these two men fills all the remaining years of British rule, but by the time independence came both were old men, too old to influence the course of events.

## The Sudan's Struggle for Independence

Following World War Two, it became clear that Britain was on the way out. In 1946, several thousand demonstrators, carrying the red, black, and green flag of the Mahdi, descended on Khartoum, demanding freedom from both Britain and Egypt. They were met by the pro-Egyptian party and there was danger of civil war.

The Umma party, founded by Sayed Abdel Rahman (el Mahdi), campaigned on the slogan, "Sudan for the Sudanese." Umma had the support of the intellectuals in the more advanced sections of the country, as well as that of the rural tribes in the west. It also had behind it the great military tradition of the Mahdi which threatened to revive the ghost of the mighty warrior who had gone down to defeat fifty years before.

The Ashigga party of Sayed Ali represented the rural vote, the sheiks who wanted to turn the clock back to the days of Egyptian rule. Most of its members barely had the qualifications of literacy. On the other hand, it attracted some surprising allies; for example, the pro-Communist railway unions in Atbara.

In these difficult circumstances, the British decided it was time to set up a Sudanese Legislative Assembly, in which the elected representatives could work out a compromise of their own. In the elections, the pro-Egyptian party boycotted the polls, but an Assembly of 75 members met for the first time in 1948. A Governor General's Council, consisting of 7 Sudanese and 5 British members, was the executive body.

The Council and Assembly governed the country for the next four troubled years. They were years of strife, as the average Sudanese in his factory, shop, tent, or farm came to realize that the day of the white man was over and he was free to rule his country as he wished. But how did he wish to rule? There was little agreement about this. Riots in the towns, strikes in the schools, and trouble with organized labor tore the Sudan apart. It seemed as though all that Britain had built up were going down in ruin.

Nevertheless, the Assembly produced a constitution providing for a House of Representatives with 97 seats and a Senate with 50. Elections were called in 1953 and the Sudan enjoyed the excitement of campaigning for the first time. The wildest promises were made by all parties, with much resulting confusion. The Umma should have had the strongest vote, but their position was weakened by the glamour of the new nationalist leader of Egypt, General Neguib, who appeared as the ally of the Egyptian party (now called the National Union party). When the votes were counted, National Union won with 50 seats in the House of Representatives, to 23 for Umma and the balance going to various splinter groups.

Logically, it should have meant that the Sudan would go to Egypt. But logic has little to do with history. In 1954, General Neguib was arrested by Colonel Nasser, a man unknown in the Sudan. Subsequently, the new

*Session of Parliament in Khartoum, the capital of the Sudan.*

ruler of Egypt declared war on the Moslem Brotherhood, imprisoning and executing many of its members. The Sudan could understand none of this. In this high desert plateau, religion is a serious matter, and both the Orthodox and the Mahdist Moslems viewed the persecution of their brother Moslems in Egypt with abhorrence. Suddenly, the lure of union with Egypt began to lose its appeal.

Parliament debated these issues long and hard and finally came to a unilateral decision. As of January 1, 1956, the Sudan would be totally independent. Neither Britain nor Egypt, each preoccupied with its own problems, raised any objection. And so, for the first time in over 130 years (since before Muhammad Ali's invasion), the people of the Sudan were free.

The first act of parliament was to form a coalition government. This showed the great common sense of the Sudanese, and the imaginative act earned the new state considerable prestige abroad. The Sudan became a member of the Arab League (it has always considered itself a part of the Middle East) and a member of the United Nations. A promising future lay ahead.

# Independence and After

## The Black Sudan

The history of the emerging states in Africa and Asia has rarely been peaceful, and the causes of strife may lie as much with the former colonial powers as with the newly free peoples. In nearly every case in Africa, the boundaries of the new nations have corresponded with the political designs of the colonial powers, but not in any way with the ethnic, racial, or linguistic boundaries of the Africans. Thus these new nations have come into being faced with frightful internal dissensions.

So it was with the Sudan. Already in 1955, before independence, there was a warning. A demonstration at the southern cotton-growing center of Nzara got out of hand. The black southerners thought they were being discriminated against by the Arab northern officials who were replacing the British in their posts. Police were outnumbered and opened fire, killing six. In a few days, all three southern provinces of Equatoria, Upper Nile, and Bahr el Ghazal were ablaze. The southern army contingents mutinied, killing their officers. In Equatoria, all towns except Juba fell to the insurgents.

The rebellion was put down with British help. The last British governor general personally promised a fair trial to all offenders, but evidently the rebels put little faith in the offer, since most of them escaped into the bush to form a guerrilla army that plagues the south to this day. And ever since, people in the Sudan have been quarreling over whom to blame.

*This policeman in Wau, southern Sudan, is a member of the Latuka tribe.*

195

It is fashionable today to blame the British. A statement given to this writer in Khartoum in 1969 by a spokesman for the Central Information Office said:

> The policy of the British administration was based on the classic precept of "divide and rule." Thus, in 1904, General Wingate, the Governor General of the Sudan, proclaimed that Arabic, which was then the language of communication between the tribes that did not speak each others' dialects, was not to be taught in southern schools. This was the beginning of intolerance in the Southern Sudan. It was not initiated by the Moslems. It was part of the policy of the British administration that made English the official language of the south.

There is, of course, something to be said for this argument. The three southern provinces cover an area of 250,000 square miles, or about a quarter of the total Sudan. Unlike the north, the south lies in the tropics

*Members of the Dinka tribe are gathering a new fiber called Kenaf, which is being tried out in southern Sudan.*

and is a land of swamps, called Sudd, interspersed with patches of open grassland. There is no overland communication (except for a recent railway line to Wau), and travel on the river is difficult. The Sudd has always been a natural barrier between south and north.

This was the country which the early explorers, Livingstone, Speke, and Baker found when they came looking for the sources of the Nile a hundred years ago. They also found the Negro peoples of these forests terrorized by the Arab slave traders, who came down from the north and carried off whole tribes for sale throughout the Middle East. Today the Arabs point out that the Europeans were equally aggressive in pursuing the slave trade at that time, and anyway, they say, slavery is no longer an Arab institution. Nevertheless, it was the British who did away with slavery when they took over the Sudan. This was the basis of their policy of separation.

Next, the Sudanese blame the missionaries for the breakdown of government in the south after independence. "In their zeal for converting their students to Christianity," said the spokesman, Fakhr ed-Din, "they disparaged everything relating to Islam or connected with the Moslem Sudanese of the north. It was the Christian missionaries, the messengers of peace, who were most responsible for sowing the seeds of division and dissent between northern and southern Sudanese." He goes on to cite "ample evidence" that the missionaries actively incited the mutiny.

It is difficult to come at the truth of these matters. Travel in the south today is highly restricted, and there is a tendency on the part of officials to organize tours for journalists that present only the government side of the story. Besides, since the expulsion of the missionaries, there is no one in the south to refute the official version of events, and in Khartoum the representatives of the various missionary societies are unwilling to talk for fear of losing their visas.

Certain facts, however, are incontestable. By 1956, only *one tenth* of the population of Equatoria, Upper Nile, and Bahr el Ghazal provinces had been Christianized according to the official figures (although the Verona Fathers Missionary Society claims half a million converts). The remainder of the 3 million southerners are mainly pagan; only 22,000

*The Anglican Cathedral at Khartoum is a reminder of fifty years of British rule.*

are Moslem. It is difficult, therefore, to see the missionaries as the evil genius of the revolution.

As for a concerted British policy to force Christianity on the south, the evidence is all the other way. The early governors (including Kitchener) were notably averse to missionary activity. Many of them belonged to the liberal intelligentsia, which at the turn of the century took a lofty atheistic view of progress and strongly disapproved of entrusting it to missionary hands. Lord Cromer, the British Minister to Egypt, thought missionaries liable to "commit follies"; Colonel Jackson, deputy to Wingate, expressed the view that "a black when converted becomes a scamp, a scoundrel, a loafer and a liar." These are views which British representatives in the Sudan have been heard to echo even today.

It was, in fact, despite official opposition that the missionaries went to work. The remarkable thing is that they accomplished so much. In nearly every town and village, there soon sprang up the churches inside neat compounds, flanked on one side by the dispensary and on the other by the school. For the missionaries took seriously Christ's charge that they were to be the teachers of mankind. It was their teaching that challenged the supremacy of a Moslem society, which so infuriated the north.

## Ibrahim Abboud

Whatever the cause of the uprising, things did not improve with independence. Out of eight hundred posts filled in the civil service by Sudanese, only four went to southerners. Southern members of parliament demanded their own regional government, and when this was denied they threatened to secede. The idea of regional government soon found an appeal with other groups in the Sudan. The Beja tribes in the eastern Sudan demanded their own government, as did the Nuba tribes in the west. The government in Khartoum panicked and turned over all power to the army.

*Partial view of the House of Parliament in Khartoum.*

That is the inside story of the coup of November 17, 1958, in which Gen. Ibrahim Abboud assumed power. That day he broadcast to the nation, promising the people just government, stability, and malice toward none. And, on the evidence, that is what he tried to give them. Cotton sales abroad boomed, rents were controlled, housing schemes initiated. Work began on a hydroelectric station at Sennar. A merchant fleet was being built in Yugoslav shipyards. International relations were good.

All these benefits, however, did not make the Sudanese happy. Freedom had been destroyed. General Abboud, an excellent and kindly man, found himself enmeshed in the web every dictator is forced to weave—oppression. The press was censored, trade unions were suppressed. Demonstrators drew long prison sentences. But, worst of all, the army was forced to embark on a policy of repression in the south.

It seems that the trouble had spread to the Yei district by 1957 and the Ministry of Defense authorized the burning of seven hundred huts. The government took over direct control of all schools. English was outlawed in the educational system, and Arabic introduced. Catholic fathers who protested these measures were arrested, and all missionaries (617 in all) were expelled from the southern Sudan. With them a considerable number of the population went into voluntary exile. In 1962 alone, the number of Sudanese refugees in Uganda and the Congo was estimated at 60,000 and in Ethiopia 25,000.

According to a government press release, the campaign against the government was led by the missions.

> Evidently it is a political organization camouflaging under Christianity to enlist maximum moral and material support. The missionaries encouraged southerners to leave the country and join the movement abroad. The deserters were efficiently handled by church authorities across the border at destination points. This indicated that a well-organized plan among the missions in the Sudan and neighbouring countries existed.

## William Deng Founds the SANU

Among the refugees was William Deng, a former assistant district commissioner. He formed a government in exile, under the name of the Sudan African National Union (SANU), with headquarters in Léopoldville (now Kinshasa) in the Congo. According to Deng, conditions in the southern Sudan were approximating civil war. Ten thousand huts and all their contents, he alleged, had been burned to the ground by northern soldiers. At least 500,000 head of cattle, sheep, and goats had been seized and taken from their owners. Northern settlers were taking land expropriated from southerners. Shopowners were squeezed out by new licensing laws. Licenses were issued to southerners only if their shops had concrete walls and corrugated iron roofs. Yet in Juba it is easy to see the shabby shops of northern merchants, who are not affected by this "concrete-and-iron license."

Says Deng, "Here is a clear case of Africans being oppressed for no other reason than because their skin pigmentation differs from that of the people who are at present wielding power. . . . We are irresistibly led to the conclusion that the [northern] aim is to destroy the African Negroid personality and identity in the Sudan and to replace it with an Arabicized and Islamized south."

## The October Revolution

The public reaction to these events in the south was the growth of a massive resistance. In 1963, a terrorist organization called the Anya-Nya made its appearance. It declared its aims in these words: "Our patience has now come to an end and we are convinced that only the use of force will bring a decision. From today on, we shall take action. We do not want mercy, and we are not prepared to give it." After that, security in the south deteriorated. Bridges were blown up, police blockhouses destroyed, convoys shot upon. In January, 1964, the Anya-Nya made a spectacular attack on the city of Wau.

The government crumpled. Bowing to popular demand, it agreed to permit public discussion of events. The students at the University of Khartoum were the first to take up the challenge. On October 22, 1964, the students demonstrated, demanding the resignation of the government. Police, always jumpy when entrusted with firearms in Khartoum, shot into the crowd, wounding nine students. One of the students died the next day. Enormous crowds assembled for the funeral. Afterward, the mob went beserk, burning and looting.

General Abboud was appalled at the strength of the opposition to his regime. Like many another soldier, he had tried to give the country stability, but he could not see that force breeds force. Now he tried to temporize, offering to fire his most unpopular henchmen. But the mob was not satisfied. Demonstrators appeared before his house and when someone fired a shot—or it may have been a car that backfired—the presidential guard replied with a fusillade, killing fourteen people and injuring many more. The general gave in.

A new government was formed, containing many left-wing elements (three out of twelve in the cabinet were Communists). The immediate task of the government was to conclude a truce in the south and to restore the economic situation and arrange for early elections. Freedom of the press was restored and the ban on political parties lifted.

## An Anti-Western Policy Is Established

But trouble was not over yet. The southern problem remained unsolved. The new government had no better solution than the old because it was unwilling to countenance the idea of regional government for the south. A round-table conference in Khartoum produced no results. Meanwhile, military activity by the Anya-Nya increased. SANU split into two factions: one in favor of separatism and the other, which was led by William Deng, advocating self-government under a federal union. When Deng was murdered, by unknown assailants, the chances for a successful compromise deteriorated.

On Sunday, December 6, 1964, a crowd of southerners, mainly laborers, went on the rampage in Khartoum. They began overturning cars and molesting northerners. Soon they met up with a crowd emerging from the football stadium. The stage was set for mayhem. Outnumbered, the southerners took refuge in the American Mission, but the building was burned to the ground and the missionaries manhandled. The Anglican bishop and his house were saved only by the courage of his staff of northern servants. But the manhunt was on for the Christians. No one will ever know how many died that day, which came to be known as Black Sunday, but many bodies were thrown in the Nile, and others picked up outside the hospital. Police made little or no effort to interfere.

Once again the official allegation is that the missionaries started it all. It is difficult to offer comment on such charges. If you believe that missionaries do this sort of thing, you will accept that version. If you do not, you will reject it. But xenophobia, the fear and suspicion of foreigners, which was so prevalent in the Mahdi's time, began to return to the Sudan. To this day, the foreign community in Khartoum, lives in some apprehension. The Greek merchants are being squeezed out by restrictions on licenses and they talk of packing up and going home after fifty years.

Foreign policy followed suit. After years of good relations with the Western world, the new government saw fit to pursue an anti-Western policy. In the Congo, active support was given to the rebels who were trying to overthrow the government. Aid was promised to a revolt against the emperor of Ethopia, another ally of the West. As the British position became more desperate in Aden, the Sudan denied airport facilities to British supply aircraft at Khartoum airport. And, in the wake of the 1967 war between Israel and the Arab states, the Sudan broke off relations with the United States.

What is the meaning of this drift? An important factor is the confrontation between the Arab states and Israel. This has exacerbated relations of all Arabs with the West, and the Sudan considers itself an Arab state. "We are quite fanatical about Palestine," young Sudanese say proudly. Hence, anyone who aids the Arabs is their friend. Anyone who opposes them is their enemy.

But other winds of change are blowing in the world today, and no nation can afford to ignore them. A dominant factor in Africa is nationalism. The emerging nations of this vast continent are trying to find their own destinies. They do not want outside interference, and any hint of Western influence is liable to be detrimental. In the future, Christianity will have to stand on its own feet in Africa as an indigenous church, owing nothing to foreign missionaries.

It is also easy to point out the influential position gained by leftists and Communists in the government after the October revolution. While ambassadors from all the Communist states, great and small, abound in Khartoum, the United Kingdom, once the mother country, is now represented by only a chargé d'affaires in an upstairs office. This seems to be a pity, since most of the modern institutions that the Sudan has inherited are Western institutions. It is a fact that under British rule the Sudan became a modern nation and knew security, prosperity, and a high degree of contentment. The British left the Sudan voluntarily and turned over all the infrastructure of government to the people. It was hoped that this would continue to bind the Sudan and the West together.

It is true that the Communists suffered a setback late in 1966 when they allegedly staged a coup to overthrow the government. The leaders of the coup (all military men) were sentenced to long prison terms and the party was outlawed. But Communism flourishes even better underground than it does in the open.

## The Democratic Republic of the Sudan

On May 25, 1969, a Revolutionary Council, led by Gen. Jaafar Muhammad al Nimery, overthrew the government in a bloodless coup and established the Democratic Republic of the Sudan. General al Nimery declared that the history of the Sudan had hitherto been "a series of catastrophes," because too many parties "with selfish motives" had been in power. He alleged that bribery and corruption were widespread and asserted that the political parties had been "satellites of imperialism."

General al Nimery declared that the Sudan would never be allowed to return to multiparty democracy, but added that "there is no opening for creation of a Communist regime." Dr. Sadiq el Mahdi, leader of the Umma party, fled to his estate on Abba Island but was arrested two days later and flung into jail—an ignominious fate for the great-grandson of the Mahdi. Leaders of the former government were held for trial, but the Minister of National Guidance stated that the laws under which they would be tried had not yet been drawn up. There is an unmistakable Alice-in-Wonderland quality about all this.

## The Sudanese People

Despite these often incomprehensible changes of the guard, life in the Sudan goes on much as it has for generations. It is a vast land that includes many peoples of different ethnic origins and widely varying stages of development. Most of them live far from Khartoum and know little of the political questions that preoccupy the newspapers.

Far away in Kordofan, you will find the Nuba tribesmen, still much as they were when Gordon rode his camel over these plains to quell the tribal wars and stop the slave trade. In the mountains southwest of El Obeid, the Nuba took refuge from the Arab slavers who roamed

*More than a million people in Bahr-el-Ghazal were vaccinated in an intensive campaign against smallpox in the early 1960's. Seen here is one of the villages in the area.*

these spaces a hundred years ago. Only in recent years have they come down to the foothills.

The Nuba total about half a million people, a thirtieth part of the population of the Sudan. Far across the desert you can see their strange clusters of round stone towers thatched with straw, each clinging to a hilltop like a medieval castle. Only when you get up close do you realize that all these smiling, friendly people are quite naked. Clothes are worn among the Nuba only for decoration, never for everyday use.

Naked they go to the fields to harvest the millet, the single crop by which they live. Harvesting is a communal affair, and they move about in laughing groups, cutting their neighbor's crop with large knives, accompanied by the womenfolk, who carry large calabashes of millet beer on their heads.

To enter a Nuba home is to become a member of the family. It may

*Members of the Dinka tribe seen cutting sisal fiber in southern Sudan.*

*Sudanese boys on the way to school in Atbara.*

take time to get on this footing, but once you are accepted, these friendly people have no reserve. They will show you the intricate system of towers built for their defense. Every house consists of five towers, built in a circle and linked with a stone wall. One tower is for sleeping, a second for chickens, goats, or pigs (with a loft for the boys, maybe), a third for cooking. Here you may see the housewife grinding the millet on the millstones. It makes a surprisingly good mush. A fourth tower serves as a granary (the girls may have this loft), and the fifth for storage.

Among the Nuba, a man may have three wives, but he will have to build a family compound for each one, complete with five towers. As a result, most of the Nuba are monogamists! They have little or no contact with the twentieth century, except for a few Arab traders who supply their matches, flashlights, and clasp knives. Otherwise, the world outside does not exist for the Nuba.

At the other end of the scale live the young Sudanese workers in their trim white bungalows on a shady street of some northern town. If you visit Atbara, you will surely meet many of these young men and women, for Atbara is an industrial town, employing many university-trained engineers, clerks, and white-collar workers. They usually speak good English and will be pleased to take you home in the evening.

*A Sudanese lathe operator making ornamental legs for a chair at a furniture factory in Wau.*

Outwardly, their lives are wholly Western—in such things as dress, furnishings, books, and even ideas. When you sit in the small living room, surrounded by the family pictures on the wall, the talk is apt to be about the high cost of living, the salaries for white-collar workers (which they say are abysmally low), and the unions, which are always calling for more strikes. (Some favor unions, some do not.)

The impression that emerges from these conversations is that life for the educated minority is still very confined in the Sudan, with few opportunities for employment. Most young people are intensely patriotic, but many of them seem anxious to get away and find a career outside the country. Although the Sudan has broken relations with the United States, American visitors will receive many inquiries about the possibility of coming to America.

Many of these young people greatly admire the West, even though they will criticize Western politics, militarism, and racial discrimination. They are hungry for books and ideas from the West, and in some way seem to blame the Western nations for not welcoming them into the Great Society.

A bridge needs to be built here, and the sooner this happens, the better it will be if the Sudanese people are to chart their future alongside the West. One of the best ways would be to initiate exchange visits between the Sudan and Western countries, and to multiply greatly the free scholarships offered in Western universities for overseas students. Even a system of letter writing between pen pals in the West and the Sudan, organized through high schools, would be of great value.

Although many girls in urban centers like Atbara are now receiving high school educations, they still do not mix with the boys for discussion on social occasions. They will meet you, however, in their own groups

*Headquarters of the local government of Equatoria Province.*

and show that they are also passionately interested in the future of their country. The first woman member of parliament was elected to the former government on a Communist ticket. Perhaps there is a message in that.

It must be recognized, nevertheless, that this is a time of retreat for Western prestige in the Sudan. As in all emerging countries, these proud and independent people want to chart their own course, make their own mistakes, and find their own solutions. We should give them all the help we can, without interference. We should offer advice and not be afraid to give criticism too, but we must recognize that this high table-land of Africa is *their* land, and wish them well in it.

Time, as we have seen, never stands still, and in the course of the next few years, great changes will come. The Sudan, the largest country in Africa, is now a nation of over 14,000,000. It still has plenty of room to expand its population. Much of its desert country can be irrigated; the Gezira cotton fields can be expanded from two to five million acres. There are great possibilities for industrial development, making use of the hydroelectric resources of the Sennar and other dams.

The Sudan is a powerhouse of the future. Will it be a friendly nation to the West, opening up its resources to Western development, and sharing in Western prosperity? Or will it turn toward alien and total-itarian solutions for its problems? A great deal depends on our own understanding of history and our willingness to build a common future with the developing nations of the earth.

# HISTORICAL HIGHLIGHTS

*Egypt*

B.C.

4241 First calendar introduced

3000 Menes unites Upper and Lower Egypt under Old Kingdom

2900 Khufu builds the Great Pyramid

2750 First Time of Troubles

2000 Middle Kingdom established by Amenemhet I

1788 Second Time of Troubles

1580 New Empire established by Ahmose I

1525 Thutmose I conquers Nubia up to Third Cataract; conquers Asia to the Euphrates River.

1503 Hatshepsut, the first woman Pharaoh

1375 Ikhnaton establishes a new religion

1304 Rameses II (the Great)

1237 Rameses II dies; Sea Peoples invade Egypt

525 Persians conquer Egypt

332 Alexander the Great conquers Egypt

51 Cleopatra becomes the second woman Pharaoh

30 Roman conquest

A.D.

324 Byzantine period begins

640 Arab conquest

876 Ibn Tulun builds the first great mosque

969 Fatimid Dynasty

970 Al-Azhar University founded

1009 Al-Hakim destroys the Church of Holy Sepulcher in Jerusalem, thereby starting the Crusades

1171 Saladin founds the Ayyubid Dynasty

1250 Mameluke Dynasty

*Sudan*

B.C.

3000 First Egyptian conquest of Nubia (Northern Sudan) under Menes

A.D.

200 The Sudan wholly Christianized by the Copts

| *Egypt* | *Sudan* |
|---|---|
| A.D. | A.D. |
| 1517 Ottoman Turks conquer Egypt | 1504 Christian states in Sudan fall to Moslem invasion |
| 1798 Napoleon takes Egypt; loses it again | |
| 1811 Muhammad Ali founds a dynasty | 1821 Muhammad Ali conquers the Sudan as far south as Darfur |
| 1869 Suez Canal opened | |
| 1882 Revolt of Colonel Arabi defeated; British rule begins | 1874 General Gordon opens up the Sudan province of Equatoria |
| | 1885 Revolt of the Mahdi takes Khartoum; Mahdi dies; is succeeded by the Khalifa |
| | 1898 The Sudan reconquered by Anglo-Egyptian force under Kitchener |
| | 1899 Condominium Government set up |
| 1922 Fuad I becomes first King of Egypt | 1922 Sudan Mutiny |
| 1936 Mutual Defense Treaty with Britain provides for British military base at Suez Canal; Farouk becomes King | 1925 Sennar Dam constructed, creating Gezira cotton industry |
| 1945 Arab League founded | |
| 1948 Egypt invades Palestine | 1948 First Legislative Assembly meets |
| 1949 Armistice with Israel | |
| 1952 Revolution of the Free Officers under General Neguib; King Farouk abdicates; Five-Year Plan for Social and Economic Development | 1953 National Union Government elected |
| 1954 Colonel Nasser deposes General Neguib | 1955 Army mutiny in Equatoria Province |
| 1956 Suez Canal nationalized; Britain, France, and Israel invade Egypt | 1956 Sudan declared independent under coalition government |
| 1958 Union of Egypt and Syria; Soviet agreement to build Aswan High Dam signed | 1958 Military coup by General Ibrahim Abboud |
| 1961 Syria withdraws from Union | 1963 Anya-Nya terrorist movement begins operation in South |
| | 1964 Government of General Abboud falls; "Black Sunday" massacres in Khartoum |
| 1967 Six-day war with Israel; Israeli Army occupies Sinai | 1966 Communist coup fails |
| 1968 First generation of electric power by Aswan High Dam | 1969 Democratic government over-thrown by military coup under Colonel Muhammad al Nimery |

# Further Reading

Aldred, Cyril, *The Egyptians.* London, Thames & Hudson, 1962.

Arnold, Sir Thomas, ed., *The Legacy of Islam.* London, Oxford University Press, 1931.

Beshir, Mohamed Omer, *The Southern Sudan.* London, C. Hurst & Co., 1968.

Breasted, James H., *A History of Egypt,* rev. ed. New York, Charles Scribner's Sons, 1937.

Burns, E. L. M., *Between Arab and Israeli.* London, George G. Harrap and Co., Ltd.

Henderson, K. D. D., *Sudan Republic.* London, Ernest Benn Ltd., 1965.

Hopkins, Harry, *Egypt the Crucible.* London, Secker & Warburg, 1969.

Little, Tom, *Modern Egypt.* London, Ernest Benn Ltd., 1965.

Ludwig, Emil, *The Nile.* London, George Allen & Unwin, 1950.

Moorhead, Alan, *The Blue Nile.* London, Hamish Hamilton, 1962.

St. John, Robert, *The Boss: A Biography of Gamal Abdel Nasser.* Toronto, McGraw-Hill Co., 1960.

# Index

Israel, 115, 124, 125, 126, 127, 130, 131, 154, 203

Jawhar (Fatimid general), 82, 85
Jordan, 115, 116, 125, 134
Juba, 184, 195

*ka,* 46
Karnak, 36, 55, 65
*kenaf,* 196
Khafre (Chephren), 28, 29
Khan el Khalili Bazaar, 85, 88
Khartoum, 165, 169, 171, 178, *198,* 202
Khartoum University, 186, 201, 202
Khufu (Cheops), 28, 29, 38
Khumarawayh (Tulunid ruler), 81
Kitchener, Horatio Herbert, earl of, 117, 178, 179, 181, 186, 198
Kordofan, 170, 205

land reform in Egypt, 123
Libya, 135
Livingstone, David, 197
Ludwig, Emil, 21
Luxor, 35, 36, 57

Macedonian Empire, 72
Mahdi, the, 170, 191
Mahdi, Dr. Sadiq el, 204
Mameluke Dynasty, 92, 97, 99, 100, 102
Manzala, Lake, 64
Maspero, Gaston, 38, 40
Memphis, 28, 30
Menes, 28
Menkure (Mycerinus), 28, 29
Middle Kingdom, 44
Mirghani, Sayed Ali, 191

Muhammad Ali, 168, 193
Mycerinus (Menkure), 28, 29

Napoleon, 99
Nassar, Dr. Said, 143
Nasser, Gamal Abdel, 120, 121, 192
Nasser, Lake, 66, 162
Nefretete (Nefertiti), 59, 61
Neguib, Mohammed, 119, 121, 123, 192
New Nubia, *98*
Nile Valley, 13
Nimery, Jaafar Muhammad al, 135, 204
*norag,* 139
Nubia, 159
Nubian Desert, 166
Nuba tribe, 205

Obeid, El, 170, 178, 183
Old Kingdom, 27, 30, 44
Old Shepheard's Hotel, 118
Om Saber, 145
Omdurman, 179, 181
    battle of, 176
Osiris, 30, 43
Ottoman Dynasty, 97

Per Ramese, 63, 64
Pharos, 72
Pompey, 73
population
    of Egypt, 149
    of the Sudan, 210
Port Said, 64, *107, 125,* 126
Port Sudan, 183
Ptolemies Dynasty, 68, 72
pyramid, 18, 28, 29, 30
    of Khafre, 24, 29

# About the Author

LARRY HENDERSON is an authority on the Middle East and is currently press officer for the Ministry of Public Information in Tanzania. As a reporter for Canadian press and television, he has visited Israel and the Arab states regularly over the past twenty years, and has produced many television documentaries about the area. He is the author of THE ARAB MIDDLE EAST and of VIETNAM AND COUNTRIES OF THE MEKONG. Of the latter book, which is part of the *World Neighbors* series, the *New York Times* reviewer wrote, "Henderson's book should be required reading at the junior high-school level. There is no proselytizing. The presence of the American in Vietnam is portrayed with great understanding. There can be no finer introduction for a child to the many different kinds of people and the way they live in Southeast Asia." The *Library Journal* reviewer said of the same book, "The author's approach is vigorous and realistic and has an obvious undercurrent of concern and idealism which should strike a responsive chord in young people."

# World Neighbors

Written to introduce the reader to his contemporaries in other lands and to sketch the background needed for an understanding of the world today, these books are well-documented, revealing presentations. Based on firsthand knowledge of the country and illustrated with unusual photographs, the text is informal and inviting. Geographical, historical, and cultural data are woven unobtrusively into accounts of daily life. Maps, working index, chronology, and bibliography are useful additions.

ALASKA: Pioneer State, by Norma Spring
THE ARAB MIDDLE EAST, by Larry Henderson
ARGENTINA, PARAGUAY & URUGUAY, by Axel Hornos
AUSTRALIA & NEW ZEALAND, by Lyn Harrington
AUSTRIA & SWITZERLAND: Alpine Countries, by Bernadine Bailey
BRAZIL: Awakening Giant, by Kathleen Seegers
CANADA: Young Giant of the North, by Adelaide Leitch
CENTRAL AFRICA: The New World of Tomorrow, by Glenn D. Kittler
CENTRAL AMERICA: Lands Seeking Unity, by Charles Paul May
CHILE: Progress on Trial, by Charles Paul May
CHINA & THE CHINESE, by Lyn Harrington
CZECHOSLOVAKIA, HUNGARY, POLAND, by Ivan & Mary Volgyes
EGYPT AND THE SUDAN: Countries of the Nile, by Larry Henderson
GERMANY: A Divided Nation, by Alma & Edward Homze
GREECE & THE GREEKS, by Lyn Harrington
INDIA: Land of Rivers, by L. Winifred Bryce
IRELAND: The Edge of Europe, by Arnold Dobrin
ISRAEL: New People in an Old Land, by Lily Edelman
ITALY: Modern Renaissance, by Arnold Dobrin
JAPAN: Crossroads of East and West, by Ruth Kirk
THE LOW COUNTRIES: Gateways to Europe, by Roland Wolseley
MEDITERRANEAN AFRICA: Four Muslim Nations, by Glenn D. Kittler
MEXICO: Land of Hidden Treasure, by Ellis Credle
PERU, BOLIVIA, ECUADOR: The Indian Andes, by Charles Paul May
SCANDINAVIA: The Challenge of Welfare, by Harvey Edwards
THE SOVIET UNION: A View from Within, by Franklin Folsom
SPAIN & PORTUGAL: Iberian Portrait, by Daniel Madden
THE UNITED KINGDOM: A New Britain, by Marian Moore
VIETNAM and Countries of the Mekong, by Larry Henderson
THE WEST INDIES: Islands in the Sun, by Wilfred Cartey
YUGOSLAVIA, ROMANIA, BULGARIA, by Lila Perl